# Teaching Christian Children about Judaism

Deborah J. Levine

*Advisor*
Sr. Mary Ellen Coombe, nds
Director, Institute for Catholic-Jewish Education
Chicago IL

Liturgy Training Publications

Acknowledgments

We are grateful to the photographers and publishers who have given permission to use their work in this book. Acknowledgments will be found at the back of this book.

The music on the audiotape is by the adult choir of Congregation Etz Chaim, Lombard, Illinois; Greg Zelman, director; Steven Bob, rabbi. It was recorded at Jor Dan Studio, Wheaton, Illinois; Glenn West, audio engineer.

The author is grateful to the following who helped critique the text and offered valuable assistance: Rabbi Peter Knobel, Beth Emet Synagogue, Evanston, Illinois; Mrs. Anne Stein, temple educator, Congregation Etz Chaim, Lombard, Illinois; Dr. Clarisse Croteau Chonka, consultant; St. Joseph's Catholic Church, Downers Grove, Illinois; DuPage Interfaith Resource Network; Rabbi Harold Kudan; Kathi Lieb, Spertus Institute of Jewish Studies, Chicago, Illinois.

This book was edited by David A. Lysik, with assistance from Deborah Bogaert, the production editor. It was designed and typeset by Jennifer Carney of Carney Design, illustrated by Laura Montenegro, and printed by BookCrafters, Chelsea, Michigan.

Library of Congress Cataloging-in-Publication Data

Levine, Deborah J.
        Teaching Christian children about Judaism / Deborah J. Levine; advisor, Mary Ellen Coombe.
                p. cm.
                Includes bibliograhpical references.
                ISBN 1-56854-076-0: $18.00
                1. Fasts and feasts—Judaism—Study and reaching (Elementary)
2. Judaism—Customs and practices—Study and teaching (Elementary)
3. Prayer— Judaism—Study and teaching (Elementary)  4. Judaism—
Relations—Christianity and other religions—Judaism—Study and teaching
(Elementary)  6. Christian education of children.  I. Coombe, Mary
Ellen.  II. Title.
BM690.L39  1995                                        94-48369
296'.07—dc20                                            CIP

CODE: TCCAJ
$18.00

# Contents

# Introduction

It is impossible to understand Christianity without reference to Judaism. The two are inextricably linked. Consider the following:

• The early followers of Jesus were Jews.

• Jews and Christians have some common scriptures.

• Judaism is the source of the Christian proclamation that God is one and that God is merciful, gracious, and in a covenantal relationship with humankind.

• Jesus was a Jew, and his words and deeds cannot be fully understood apart from an understanding of first-century Palestinian Jewish life.

• Christian worship, especially the eucharist, finds its roots in Jewish liturgical life.

As Pope John Paul II said in 1982, Christianity and Judaism are "linked together at the very level of their identity."

Yet the relationship between Jews and Christians throughout history often has been a troubled one. In the first century, Christianity was still a movement *within* Judaism, although the early development of its distinctive liturgy can be seen in the writings of Saint Paul. The "parting of ways" took place gradually, and it was not until the middle of the fourth century that Christianity and Judaism were clearly separate and distinct religions. Before this complete separation, however, many of the New Testament and patristic polemics against Jews and Judaism were composed and circulated. These polemics reflected the confrontations between the emerging church and the developing rabbinic tradition, both of which were concerned with issues of group identity and appropriate lines of demarcation.

At the end of the fourth century, Christianity was established as the official religion of the Roman Empire. During the following centuries, in consolidating its secular power, the church was ambivalent in its policy toward the Jews. On the one hand, it sought to suppress the attractiveness of Judaism to potential converts. On the other hand, it desired to protect the existence of Judaism as a witness to the validity of the Hebrew Bible, upon which Christian proclamation is based. The teachings of contempt against Jews and Judaism, initially only theoretical, became concrete in such tragic acts against Jews as forced exile, forced baptism, Talmud burnings, blood libels and consignment to ghettos. Beginning in the tenth century, the Crusaders perpetrated violent acts against the Jewish communities of Christian Europe, despite the opposition of the pope. By the end of the sixteenth century, the Jewish communities of Western Europe were decimated.

From the Enlightenment to the eve of World War II, Jews were gradually freed from the ghettos and some contributed significantly to European culture and society. However, much of European society still considered Jews to be "outsiders." During this time, a pseudo-scientific racism developed and Nazism carried this theory to its most extreme to justify the Holocaust, in which, ultimately, two-thirds of the Jews in Europe were systematically murdered.

The shock of realizing what had happened began with the liberation of the Nazi death camps by the Allied armies. When a Jewish state was established in the land of Israel, the Jewish people renewed their ability to hope. A spirit of hope for the future grew within the Catholic church as well, bearing fruit in *Nostra Aetate*, the Second Vatican Council's *Declaration on the Relation of the Church to Non-Christian Religions*. Similar statements have also been issued by other churches.

For almost 2000 years the dominant understanding of the relationship between Christianity and Judaism was that Judaism had been supplanted by Christianity. Judaism represented the old covenant, and Christianity the new. Judaism's rule of law was contrasted with the sovereignty of love preached by Jesus, a view which argued that the church had made Judaism obsolete, unnecessary.

*Nostra Aetate*, promulgated in 1965, points the way for a new approach. It uses the imagery of St. Paul in Romans 9 to say that the church is grafted onto the tree of salvation whose trunk is Judaism. This implies a continuing life for Judaism, for if the trunk has died the branches can hardly remain healthy. *Nostra Aetate* also puts to rest the false teaching that the Jewish people are eternally guilty for the crime of killing Jesus ("deicide"). This false notion has been responsible for the persecution of many, many Jews throughout history. The final section of *Nostra Aetate* also repudiates anti-Semitism as incompatible with the gospel.

Since 1965, many Catholic and Protestant statements have been issued at all levels of church life. There have been significant changes in liturgy and in education materials. All of this activity has helped the church not only to realize that the recovery of the spirit and teachings of biblical Judaism is vital for a healthy Christianity, but also to recognize Judaism as an ongoing, vigorous tradition that stands independent of Christianity. The next step involves integrating these teachings into the everyday life of the church and providing Christian adults and children with an experience of the life of Judaism.

This book begins to take this next step. One of its key elements is to provide education on many levels with an emphasis on the experiential, not just on the intellectual component of learning. Through music, art, stories and sacred objects, students are guided briefly into the Jewish world. And even though this book is primarily geared to the education of young students, it can also be meaningful to others; many people in the Christian community are unfamiliar with Judaism and Jewish life. Experience not only promotes an understanding of Judaism, it also sharpens an appreciation of the student's and the adult's Christian heritage.

If there is a Jewish community in your neighborhood, it would be a very good idea to invite some of its members to work with you in presenting the material in these lessons. However, if this is not possible, use these lessons to help you and your students discover the vitality of Jewish life today.

# How to Use This Book

There are seven lessons in this book. Originally designed for use in grades one through eight in Catholic elementary schools, the material can easily be adapted to other grades and a variety of Christian settings.

With younger students, this book can be used by assigning one lesson per grade. However, this plan should be coordinated so that a student in the first grade will proceed through the program experiencing a different lesson in each grade. An alternate strategy is to use all seven lessons in one grade over the period of a school year.

A good starting place with older students is the lesson entitled "The Liturgical Year." The liturgical year itself can then guide the use of the other lessons. The lessons on specific holidays can be coordinated to coincide with the appropriate season: the lesson on Rosh Hashanah (the Jewish New Year) and Yom Kippur in September–October; the lesson on scripture in the Fall to coincide with Simhat Torah; the lesson on Hanukkah in December; the lesson on Passover in April–May. The lesson on the synagogue can be coordinated with a field trip to a local synagogue. The lesson on prayer and the Sabbath can be used when most convenient.

## How to Use Each Lesson

### A. Preparing a Lesson

Background information is included with each lesson. The teacher or leader should read this background material in preparation for the class. The teacher should also read the question and answer section *before* presenting the material in class. This section features frequently asked questions, along with suggested answers. Familiarity with the background information and the question and answer section will enable the teacher to guide the discussion.

### B. Lesson Plan

Each lesson has a suggested lesson plan that often contains additional information to be read along with the background material. Some lesson plans require the use of the accompanying audiotape, the appropriate use of which is noted in the plan.

### C. Student's Take Home Page

Each lesson has a page that can be photocopied for the students to take home and share with their parents or keep as a quick reminder of the lesson. The Take Home pages are visual aids using pictures and brief phrases. Also included is a Parent's Summary Page in which the background information for that lesson is summarized. This page can be copied and sent home with the student to share with his or her parent(s). In this way, parents can share the classroom experience of their children.

On some Take Home pages there are Hebrew words and phrases. Below the Hebrew letters is an English transliteration that provides the approximate sound of the Hebrew. Practice with the transliteration in class to give the students some experience of the sound of Hebrew.

## D. Glossary

The glossary is a convenient reference source for terms found in the book.

## E. Resources

Teachers and leaders can pursue topics covered in the lessons beyond the information provided. The resource appendix contains a selected bibliography to facilitate additional research. In addition, a list of mail-order suppliers of Jewish education materials is provided.

# Introducing a Lesson

Some students have had minimal exposure to Judaism and see little reason to study it. The teacher or leader will need to prepare the students for the material by establishing a context for the lesson. The lessons in this book can be taught by a Christian teacher in the absence of a representative of the Jewish community. However, this book was designed for optimal use in a team teaching setting, where the Christian team member would make the introduction to the lesson and the Jewish team member would teach the background material and field questions about Judaism.

## A. Introductions

When a team is teaching the class, the Christian team member begins with a personal introduction followed by an introduction of the Jewish team member. If it is not possible to form a team, then teachers should discuss their personal interest in studying Judaism.

## B. What does "Jewish" mean?

After this brief personal introduction, the Christian teacher should help the students make connections by asking such questions as: Do you know any Jews? Where did you meet them? Students in grades one through three may not know what it means to be Jewish. Students in grades one through six may not have made the connection between Jewish and Judaism, nor recognized that Judaism is a religion. Establishing a context for learning about Judaism requires building on a recognizable common denominator, the Bible. The teacher should remind the students that there are Jewish people in the Bible. The teacher should then ask the students if they can name any of them, writing the names suggested on the blackboard as indicated below.

## C. What is the difference between Christians and Jews?

Divide the list of biblical names into "Jewish People in the Old Testament" and "Jewish People in the New Testament." This list will help define the formative stories of Judaism and Christianity. Judaism centers around the story of creation, the Exodus and the Promised Land; Christianity centers on the story of Jesus and his teachings and the life of the early church. Refer to this list when speaking of traditions and rituals that pertain to either the Jewish story or the Christian story.

| Jewish People in the Old Testament | Jewish People in the New Testament |
| --- | --- |
| Noah | Elizabeth |
| Abraham | Mary |
| Sarah | Joseph |
| Isaac | John the Baptist |
| Rebecca | Jesus |
| Jacob | the Apostles |
| Esau | Matthew |
| Rachel | Mark |

| Jewish People in the Old Testament | Jewish People in the New Testament |
|---|---|
| Leah | Luke |
| Moses | John |
| Miriam | Mary Magdalene |
| Joshua | Martha |
| David | Thomas |
| Solomon | Peter |
| Samuel | Peter |

Throughout the lessons, you will notice the students working to understand the differences between Christianity and Judaism. Initially, the students will work to understand that Judaism and Christianity are different religions. Younger Christian students are just beginning to identify with their own tradition and often find it difficult to make the connection that, for example, Jews do not celebrate Christmas or Easter.

It is sometimes helpful to return to the names and the stories in both the Old and New Testaments, defining for the students the formative stories of Judaism and Christianity: for Judaism, the stories of creation, the Exodus and the Promised Land; for Christianity, the stories of Jesus and the early church. The traditions and rituals of a religion help the community to remember and celebrate the central stories of its religion. Thus, for example, as part of remembering the Christian story, Christians celebrate the birth of Jesus. But this event is not a part of the Jewish story; hence Jews do not celebrate Christmas.

## D. Who are Jews today?

The next step is to establish a connection with contemporary Jews. Ask the students if they know any Jews. Teachers should note that the field-testing of this manual has shown that some children in parochial schools have Jewish relatives in their families. Other children may have Jewish neighbors. If no one in the class has any Jewish connections, the teacher may wish to draw on television and movies.

## E. Why should we learn about Judaism and Jewish people? Why does the church ask us to do this?

• They are friends, neighbors and sometimes relatives.
• The Jewish community has suffered from the prejudice of others. The task of education is to break down stereotypes and foster understanding.
• Jesus and many of his followers were Jewish. Learning about Judaism promotes a better understanding of Christianity.
• The Old Testament (Hebrew Scriptures) is the story of the Jewish people. The part of the Bible we call the Old Testament is the whole Bible for the Jews.

## F. Specific topic

The preparation for the lesson is completed with the introduction of the specific topic. The teacher can use the introduction given with each lesson to present the topic, share background information and implement the lesson plan(s).

## Lesson 1

# The Liturgical Year

## Introduction

The liturgical year tells the story of a religious community. Religious festivals, celebrations and commemorations define the community's sacred space, time and history. Judaism has been a model for many religions, including Christianity, on how to create and affirm the religious life of the community through the use of a liturgical calendar. By studying the Jewish calendar, Christians can better understand the development of their own liturgical calendar and its role in shaping their faith.

## Background

The Torah is read each year from beginning to end, and the ancient story is woven into the seasons of the year and the gift of God's creation. Genesis begins with the story of God creating the world in six days, resting on the seventh. Therefore, the week has seven days. The day begins at sundown so that God's miracle of creating light from darkness is appreciated every day of the week. The Jewish calendar is dated from the Jewish understanding of the world's beginning and is over 5,000 years old. Jewish months are measured by the moon and do not coincide exactly with the dates of secular months. Jewish months are shorter than our secular months, and an extra month—a leap month—is added to the calendar seven times within a nineteen year period.

The ancient Jewish community was one of farmers and shepherds, and their customs are reflected in the Jewish calendar. There are three major harvest festivals, one in spring (Passover), one in summer (Shavuot), and one in the fall (Sukkot). These holidays once included pilgrimages during which a portion of the harvest was offered to God at the Temple in Jerusalem. Since the Temple was destroyed centuries ago, the harvest/pilgrimage rituals have been adapted for use in the home and synagogue.

In addition to having seasonal themes, Jewish holidays also have biblical and religious themes. Sukkot comes in the fall and is linked to thanksgiving for the bounty of the fields. Members of the community, or individual families, build a *sukkah* in which they live, study or eat for the holiday. A *sukkah* is a temporary dwelling, a hut or booth with four sides and with slats for a roof that permit a view of the stars. The *sukkah* is finely decorated with vegetables, fruit, wreaths of corn, paper chains and pictures of Jerusalem. Israelite farmers would live in these booths for days during the harvest. Today, the *sukkah* is still built to remind Jews of their roots in the Promised Land of the covenant. Sukkot is a time of joyous thanksgiving, celebrating God's generosity to all people. Many Jews believe that the messiah will come during Sukkot, a time of abundance and beauty.

Passover comes in the spring and expresses joy in new life. The egg and parsley of the Passover Seder meal harken back to the seasonal meaning of the holiday. However, Passover is also based on the story of Exodus and underscores religious freedom. (See lesson four on Passover.)

Forty-nine days from the second night of Passover is the harvest holiday called Shavuot, which also commemorates Moses receiving the Torah at Mount Sinai. The celebration of this holiday includes studying the Torah and honoring religious education.

The Jewish year begins with a communal gathering at the new year, Rosh Hashanah. The beginning of a new year marks ten days of solemn reflection by the community on humanity's place in God's creation: to honor God's work as human beings and as Jews. The traditions and laws of the Torah and the centuries of commentaries on the Torah are beloved and revered for the ways they shape Jewish identity and allow the Jewish community to honor God. As the Christian liturgical year links Christians with Jesus, the Jewish holy days link the Jewish people to the Torah, the Promised Land and their covenant with God.

## Lesson Plan

1. Review "Introducing a Lesson" on pages 5–6. If needed, use the material found there to begin the class.

2. The theme of this lesson is how our liturgical calendars celebrate our stories. Discuss some of the Christian holy days throughout the year—especially the Easter Triduum, Pentecost, Christmas and Epiphany—and how they help us to be a part of the life of Jesus.

3. Discuss how the Jewish liturgical calendar illustrates a Jewish understanding of creation. Note how the day and the week are structured on the story of Genesis. It is also significant that the Jewish day begins at sundown. Talk about how the Jewish holidays observe seasons as well as biblical and religious themes—e.g., Passover commemorates the spring harvest *and* the story of Exodus; Sukkot celebrates the fall harvest *and* the Promised Land; Shavuot celebrates the summer bounty *and* Moses' reception of the Torah.

4. Distribute copies of the "Take Home Page" to the class. Use it in your discussion of the Jewish holidays.

5. Discuss Sukkot. Invite your Jewish teaching partner to tell how he or she celebrates this feast. Show the photo of a *sukkah* (page 10) to the class. Read about this feast in the Bible in Leviticus 23: 39-43.

## Additional Plans

1. Examine a Jewish calendar and compare it with the secular calendar. Note how the names of the months and the date of the year differ. The Jewish months are: Nisan, Iyar, Sivan, Tammuz, Av, Elul, Tishrei, Heshvan, Kislev, Tevet, Shevat, Elul, Adar, and Adar II (in leap years). January 1, 1995 is Shevat 1, 5755 in the Jewish calendar. July 1, 1995 is Tammuz 14, 5756.

## Audiotape

The audiotape for this lesson contains:
"Halelujah," by Lewandowski (2:30).
The traditional "Give thanks on Sukot day" (0:20).
Two traditional Purim songs, "A Wicked Man" (1:47) and "Utsu Eitsa" (0:52)

# Questions and Answers

*1. How do Jewish people celebrate Sukkot?*

The fall festival, Sukkot, is celebrated by building booths (*sukkah*) out of wood and branches and by hanging fruits and vegetables like squash and gourds from the slats of the roof. For the seven or eight days (traditions vary) of Sukkot, Jews eat and pray in the *sukkah*, under the stars, as Jews did during the ancient harvests.

*2. What relationship does Sukkot have to the American Thanksgiving?*

Sukkot is the celebration of thanksgiving for the Promised Land. When the pilgrims landed in North America, they felt like the Israelites who gained their freedom from Egypt. The pilgrims knew the Bible well, and modeled their Thanksgiving on Sukkot.

*3. How do Jewish people celebrate Shavuot?*

Shavuot is mainly celebrated by studying religion and its ethical obligations. The holiday is associated with the gift of the Torah.

*4. Why do Jewish holidays come at different times each year?*

The Jewish holidays actually come at the same time each year according to the Jewish calendar. However, because the Jewish calendar is a lunar one, the Jewish months do not coincide with our secular months and so appear to move.

*5. Why do Jewish holidays start at sunset?*

In ancient times, there was no electricity. When darkness fell, the holiday with its lighting of candles was a special time commemorating the gift of God's creation from nothingness, light from the darkness.

*6. Why don't you ever see AD after Jewish dates?*

AD means *anno Domini*—"in the year of the Lord"—and refers to Jesus Christ. Since Jesus is not a central figure in Judaism, references to his life are not used in Jewish calendars. Yet, given the reliance on a secular calendar that does use this dating system, some accommodation has been made. Jews use the terminology Common Era (CE) and Before the Common Era (BCE) in instances where some non-Jews use AD and BC.

The synagogue is where the Jewish community gathers for prayer. Notice the large menorah on the left and the ark containing the Torah scrolls over by the stained-glass window.

This is the inside of a *sukkah*. On the feast of Sukkot, Jews build these temporary dwellings and decorate them with branches, fruit and pictures. Sukkot is a time of thanksgiving for God's generosity to all people.

# The Liturgical Year

When Jews celebrate their holidays throughout the year, they remember two things:
First, they remember the ancient stories of the Jewish people as written in the Bible.
Second, they also celebrate the seasons and remember the gifts of God's creation.

Here is a list of some of the important Jewish holidays:

*Sabbath*
the weekly day of prayer and study, celebrated from sunset Friday to sunset Saturday.

*Rosh Hashanah*
the Jewish New Year.

*Yom Kippur*
the holiest day in the Jewish year, it is a day of fasting and prayer.

*Sukkot*
the joyful thanksgiving festival of the fall harvest.

*Simhat Torah*
the holiday to celebrate the Torah.

*Hanukkah*
the wintertime celebration of the rededication of the Temple in Jerusalem; also called
the Festival of Lights.

*Passover*
the springtime celebration of the exodus of the ancient Jews from Egypt.

*Shavuot*
the summer harvest festival that also remembers the receiving of the
Torah with its Ten Commandments at Mount Sinai.

# Parent's Summary • The Liturgical Year

The liturgical year, with its festivals, celebrations and commemorations, defines the community's sacred space, time and history. Judaism has been a model for many religions, including Christianity, on how to create and affirm the religious life of the community through the use of a liturgical calendar.

The ancient Jewish community was one of farmers and shepherds, and their customs are reflected in the Jewish calendar. There are three major harvest festivals: one in spring (Passover), one in summer (Shavuot), and one in the fall (Sukkot). These holidays once included pilgrimages during which a portion of the harvest was offered to God at the Temple in Jerusalem. Since the Temple was destroyed centuries ago, the harvest/pilgrimage rituals have been adapted for use in the home and synagogue.

These seasonal celebrations are also linked to a biblical/religious theme. The Torah is read each year from beginning to end and the ancient story is woven into the seasons of the year and the gift of God's creation. As the Christian liturgical year links Christians to Jesus, the Jewish holy days link the Jewish people to the Exodus, the Promised Land and the Torah.

## Lesson 2

# Rosh Hashanah and Yom Kippur

Rosh Hashanah, the Jewish New Year's Day, comes on the evening of the new moon of the new year and celebrates another year of life. Rosh Hashanah is a solemn occasion as well as a festive one. The new year begins with the Ten Days of Awe, ending with the Day of Atonement, Yom Kippur. Rosh Hashanah and Yom Kippur are also called the High Holy Days. These holy days are the most sacred times of the year, when the Jewish community celebrates God's gift of life while striving to make itself worthy of such a gift.

## Background

The Jewish New Year's Day, Rosh Hashanah, begins the Ten Days of Awe, during which Jews as a community examine their actions and intentions over the past year. This is a time of collective contemplation on the actions of the community and its responsibilities as a people in covenant with God. In keeping the commandments, Jews come closer to God and the Jewish peoplehood. Each Jew should remember the fragile nature of life. Each person must right the wrongs they have committed so that they may be judged as righteous human beings and good Jews. Have they obeyed the Ten Commandments and other laws? Have they tried to right the wrongs they may have done to others? If they were to die tomorrow, would they be judged as righteous and pious Jews?

In ancient times, the new year was announced by the sound of the *shofar* (ram's horn) being blown. The *shofar* is still blown in synagogues all over the world to call Jews to prayer and to celebrating the Jewish New Year. The *shofar* is an ancient symbol connected to the hope of messianic redemption. When the messiah comes, the *shofar* will announce the resurrection of the dead and call all Jews to prayer in Jerusalem. While Jews do not believe that Jesus was the messiah, the concept of the messiah has been a theme in Judaism since biblical times.

Yom Kippur concludes the Ten Days of Awe. On this Day of Atonement, the Jewish community fasts to purify itself and to set apart the experience of repentance from ordinary days. Thus, Jews share in the suffering of all those past and present who suffer, appreciating the sacrifices made. A traditional melody, *Kol Nidre*, sung in every synagogue, puts these lamentations in musical form. At the end of Yom Kippur, the community breaks the fast together and celebrates the opportunity to begin again.

The underlying themes of the High Holy Days are repentance, redemption and the renewal of God's gift of life. These themes, part of Judaism since a time when society was agricultural and related closely to the land and the seasons, have developed differently in Christianity and in Judaism. Yet, the understanding of the gift of life as coming from God and the struggle to be worthy of this gift have remained important elements of both religions.

# Lesson Plan

1. Review "Introducing a Lesson" on pages 5–6. If needed, use the material found there to begin the class.

2. The theme of this lesson is "living out God's covenant." Discuss the Ten Commandments. Discuss Lent as a time of year when Christians ask themselves if they have been living the way God asks them to. Discuss what Christians do during Lent.

3. Discuss what Rosh Hashanah means to the Jewish people and how they celebrate it. Invite the Jewish teaching partner, if available, to lead this discussion.

4. Talk about the *shofar*. Show the photos from this lesson. Listen to the audiotape of a *shofar* being blown. Discuss what feelings the students get from the sound of the *shofar*.

5. Cut up apples and dip them in honey for a traditional Jewish New Year's snack. Discuss why the sweetness of the honey and the fruit are good symbols of life.

6. Distribute copies of the "Take Home Page" to the class. Point out the Hebrew phrase "L'Shanah Tovah"—"A Good New Year"—and introduce the students to the Hebrew letters. Practice saying "L'Shanah Tovah."

# Additional Plans

1. Discuss what happens as we anticipate the arrival of a New Year and what happens on New Year's Eve on December 31st. Underscore the tradition of making New Year's resolutions and draw the parallel to the Jewish New Year.

2. Listen to the solemn music of *Kol Nidre* on the audiotape and discuss why Jews fast on Yom Kippur.

3. Older children can discuss the following poem.

## Holy Days
*by Valerie Worth*

Suddenly, in the
Midst of everything
New-paved cities,
Calm suburban
Gardens, endless
Acres of corn-

There rise these
Palms, these deserts,
These bitter herbs:
These ancient days
Called up by the
Ram's echoing horn.

# Audiotape

The audiotape for this lesson contains:
*"Avinu Malkeynu,"* by Max Janowski (1:19).
Traditional *Kol Nidre* chant (5:12).
The sound of a *shofar* being blown (1:46).
*"Al Cheyt* [Confession of Sin]," by Max Janowski (2:58).
Traditional New Year's greeting (1:09)

# Questions and Answers

*1. What sound does the* shofar *make?*

The *shofar* makes a sound that cuts through the congregation in loud, clear blasts. The sounds are blown in rhythms, beginning with a long blast. Then there are three short blasts and nine staccato ones. There is a long final blast that symbolizes the unity of the community and the sense of completeness one gets from prayer.

*2. Who blows the* shofar?

Members of the synagogue may blow the *shofar,* but it takes much practice to get it right. Blowing the *shofar* is considered both an honor and a great achievement.

*3. Why do Jews eat apples and honey when they celebrate their new year?*

Apples are a symbol of life, knowledge and abundance. Honey is sweet and is a special treat. Together, the apples and honey are a good metaphor for a good life. The use of foods to celebrate life is a common theme in Judaism.

*4. Why is the* Kol Nidre *music on the Day of Atonement so sad?*

*Kol Nidre* is a musical lament in which the Jewish people are reminded of the fragility of life and the obligation to make life full of goodness. *Kol Nidre* is part of the ritual renewal of life, covenant and faith. The congregation accepts the possibility of death and the life-giving nature of religion.

*5. What do Jews eat during Yom Kippur?*

Jews fast on Yom Kippur and abstain from all food and drink. Children under thirteen and those physically unable to fast are exempted.

*6. What do Jewish people wear on Rosh Hashanah?*

When Jews gather in the synagogue on Rosh Hashanah and Yom Kippur (the High Holy Days), they wear new, good clothes to start a new year. Many Jews like to wear their best clothes when they gather in the synagogue on the High Holy Days.

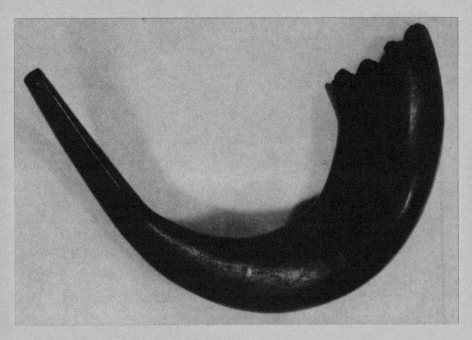

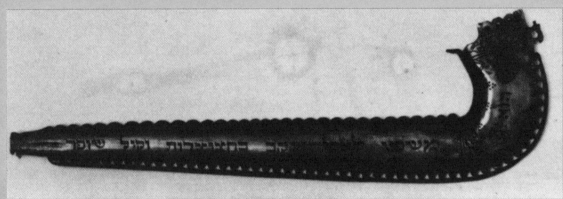

The *shofar* is a ram's horn. It makes a special sound and is used to celebrate the Jewish New Year.

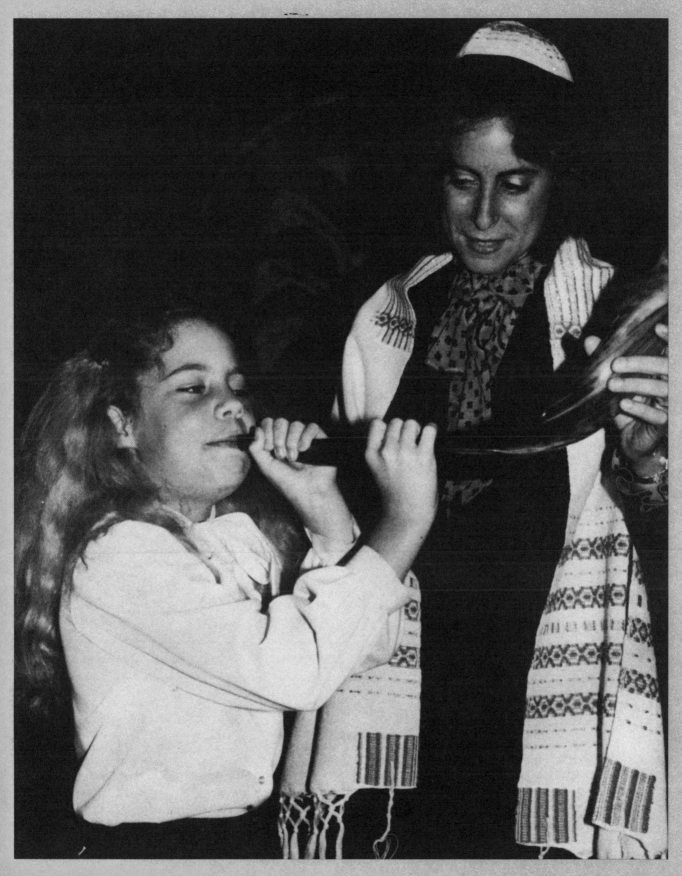

The *shofar* is used to call the people to prayer. Blowing the *shofar* is considered an honor and a great achievement.

Members of the synagogue may blow the *shofar*, but it takes
practice to get it right.

# Rosh Hashanah and Yom Kippur

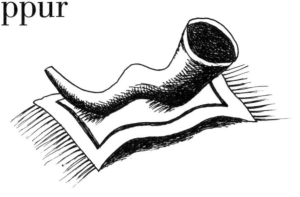

*The* shofar *is a ram's horn. It is blown to call Jews to prayer and to celebrate the Jewish New Year.*

Rosh Hashanah, the Jewish New Year's Day, is the beginning of the most sacred time of the year for Jewish people. It is the beginning of the High Holy Days. The *shofar* is blown to call the Jews to prayer. The community gathers in the synagogue to remember God's gift of life and to ask forgiveness if they have not kept God's commandments.

Here is a new year's greeting in Hebrew:

לשנה טובה

It is pronounced: "L'Shanah Tovah"

It means: "A Good New Year"

# Parent's Summary Page • Rosh Hashanah and Yom Kippur

Rosh Hashanah, the Jewish New Year's Day, comes on the evening of the new moon of the new year and celebrates another year of life. Rosh Hashanah is a solemn occasion as well as a festive one. The new year begins with the Ten Days of Awe, ending with the Day of Atonement, Yom Kippur. Rosh Hashanah and Yom Kippur are also called the High Holy Days. These holy days are the most sacred times of the year.

The Jewish community celebrates God's gift of life while it strives to make itself worthy of such a gift. Each Jew should remember the fragile nature of life. Each person must right the wrongs they have committed so that they may be judged as righteous human beings and good Jews. Have they obeyed the Ten Commandments and other laws? Have they tried to right the wrongs done to others?

In ancient times, the new year was announced by the sound of the *shofar* (ram's horn) being blown. The *shofar* is still blown in synagogues all over the world to call Jews to prayer. The underlying themes of the High Holy Days are repentance, redemption and renewal of God's gift of life. These themes, part of Judaism since a time when society was related closely to the land and the seasons, have developed differently in Judaism and in Christianity. Yet, the understanding of the gift of life coming from God and the struggle to be worthy of this gift have remained important elements of both religions.

## Lesson 3

# Hanukkah

## Introduction

Many Jewish holidays commemorate events invested with historical and religious meaning. Hanukkah means "dedication," and it commemorates the rededication of the Temple in Jerusalem after its desecration by foreign forces. The celebration also reaffirms the continuing struggle to live by God's commandments and to lead Jewish lives. This lesson on Hanukkah focuses on the *menorah*, a public symbol of God's presence with the Jewish people.

## Background

The story of Hanukkah is the struggle for religious freedom. Over a thousand years ago, the foreign rulers of the Israelites decreed that the Jews bow down to the image of their leader, Antiochus, whose statue was erected in the Temple. But the Jewish people were forbidden by the law of God to bow to statues or idols. Inspired by Mattathias and led by his son, Judah, a small group of Jews called Maccabees (meaning "hammer") rebelled. The Maccabees risked their lives to live according to Jewish law and to prevent this desecration of their sacred Temple.

Although the Maccabees won, the Temple in Jerusalem, the Jews' holy place, was destroyed. The Jews had to clean and repair the Temple, and when they were finished they rededicated it to God by rekindling the *menorah*, the nine-branched candelabrum symbolizing the eternal covenant between God and the Jewish people and the continuity of tradition through the generations. But there was only enough olive oil to fuel the *menorah* for one night, and it would have taken eight days to make more oil. The legend of the miracle at Hanukkah says that the one day supply of oil burned for eight days and nights until more oil could be made.

There are eight days of Hanukkah corresponding to the legend of the miracle of the oil in the Temple. Foods cooked in oil are traditional, particularly potato pancakes, called *latkes*. Today, candles are used instead of oil. On each successive night, the number of candles lit increases by one. Prayers accompany the lighting of the candles. (For prayers, refer to the audiotape and the student's Take Home Page for this lesson.)

Hanukkah is celebrated in the home beginning on the 25th day of the Jewish month of Kislev. Even though it is not mentioned in the Hebrew Scriptures, Hanukkah is widely celebrated as a major holy day of the Jewish liturgical calendar. Given its proximity to Christmas, Hanukkah has taken on importance in this and many other countries where Christmas has been commercialized.

It is traditional to give small gifts to children on each night of Hanukkah. The party atmosphere is enhanced with songs, games and toys such as a *dreydel*—a spinning top. A traditional favorite Hanukkah song, "A little dreydel," is found on the audiotape. Yet the religious celebration—the lighting of the candles with accompanying prayers—must come before the party.

# Lesson Plan

1. Review "Introducing a Lesson" on pages 5–6. If needed, use the material found there to begin the class.

2. Tell the story of Hanukkah. (Invite the Jewish partner, if available, to do this.)

3. Tell how Hanukkah is celebrated today in a Jewish home. (The Jewish partner, if available, should lead this presentation.)

4. Play a game of *dreydel*. The *dreydel* is a spinning top with four sides and is a very ancient toy/game. On each side is a different letter in Hebrew. The letters stand for the first word in the phrase *Nes Gadol Haya Sham*, which means, "A great miracle happened there." (*Dreydels* are widely available in larger cities during Hanukkah. See page 000 for mail-order information if you cannot find *dreydels* in your area.)

   Arrange students in small circles sitting on the floor. Give each student ten counters, such as dry beans, peanuts or shells. Each student puts one counter in the center. The students then take turns spinning the *dreydel*, playing according to the letter that shows when the top stops. (The *dreydel* will not spin on carpet.) The rules of the game are summarized by the Hebrew letters on the dreydel. Write these letters on the blackboard:

   נ = nun (put in or take nothing)

   ג = gimmel (take all)

   ה = hay (take half)

   ש = shin (put in one)

The game is over when one player has collected all the counters. Divide the counters among all the players to start the game over.

5. Demonstrate *menorah* candle lighting. The audiotape may be used to provide suitable music. (The Jewish partner can bring a *menorah* and demonstrate. If you need a *menorah*, local Jewish religious goods stores will have some in stock, or see page 74 for mail-order information.)

# Additional Plans

1. Draw a *menorah*: Make an eight-branch candelabrum with a ninth candle (shammas) larger or different than the others and used to light them. Orange and yellow tissue paper may be used to make the flames for the candles.

2. Make flash cards with Hanukkah symbols such as the *menorah*, the *dreydel*, Hebrew letters, a six-point star of David, Maccabees.

3. Attend a Hanukkah party at a synagogue or Jewish home.

4. Look at a Hanukkah storybook with pictures. (Consult the resource list at the back of this book for suggested titles and distributors of Hanukkah storybooks.)

# Audiotape

The audiotape for this lesson contains:
The folktunes "A little dreydel" (0:20) and "I'm a dreydel" (0:10).
A Hanukkah candle blessing (1:35).

# Questions and Answers

## 1. Do you speak Hanukkah?

Young children may know of Jews only through Hanukkah. Some realize that Judaism has a different language, but they confuse the holiday with the religion and its language. Hanukkah is only a single Hebrew word meaning "dedication" in English. Hebrew letters are on the *dreydel*. Hebrew is the language spoken in Israel. Also, Hebrew is the sacred language of prayer and worship.

## 2. Is Hanukkah the holiday when Jewish children receive gifts?

Traditionally, Jewish children receive small gifts only, perhaps one for each of the eight nights. Small, practical articles such as clothing, books and candy are common gifts. Many families give small amounts of money, called *gelt*. Today, gold-wrapped chocolate coins, not real money, are often used as *gelt*.

## 3. Do adults play dreydel, *too?*

The whole family joins in playing *dreydel*, not just the children.

## 4. What is a Jewish star?

The Jewish star, or *Mogen David*, is a six-point star that symbolizes the Jewish people. It is made with two triangles and adorns the flag of the state of Israel. During World War II, the Nazis made Jews wear a Jewish star on their clothing because they hated and feared them and wanted to recognize them quickly.

## 5. Do Jews celebrate birthdays? With gifts?

Jews do celebrate birthdays and receive presents on that day.

## 6. How long do the Hanukkah candles burn?

The candles burn until they are used up, which takes about an hour. Out of respect for God, the source of all light, candles are not blown out in Jewish tradition. Fresh candles are used each night of the celebration. The nine-branched Hanukkah *menorah* is special and is used only for this ritual.

The Hanukkah menorah has nine candles—eight of them for the eight days of Hanukkah and one extra candle that is used to light the others. On each night of Hanukkah the number of candles lit increases by one until all are lit on the eighth night.

Hanukkah is a happy celebration, complete with songs, games and toys. One popular Hanukkah toy is the *dreydel*—a spinning top. The *dreydel* game is a very ancient one that Jewish children still play today.

# Hanukkah

The story of Hanukkah is the story of the struggle for the freedom to be Jewish and to practice the Jewish religion. In ancient times, the Maccabees risked their lives to follow Jewish law and to save the Temple. They won the battle, but the Temple was destroyed. When the Jews cleaned and repaired the Temple and wanted to light the *menorah*, there was only enough oil for it to burn for one day. But when it was lit, it burned for eight days! That is the great miracle of Hanukkah.

Prayer over the Hanukkah candles:

בָּרוּךְ אַתָּה, יְיָ אֱלֹהֵינוּ, מֶלֶךְ הָעוֹלָם, אֲשֶׁר קִדְּשָׁנוּ
בְּמִצְוֹתָיו, וְצִוָּנוּ לְהַדְלִיק נֵר שֶׁל חֲנֻכָּה:

Ba-rooch a-ta a-do-nai, el-o-hey-nu me-lech ha-o-lam,
a-sher kid-shah-nu b'mitz-vo-tah, v'tzee-va-nu l'had-leek
ner, shel Ha-nuk-kah.

Blessed are you, Lord our God, King of the Universe,
who has blessed us with the commandments
and commanded us to light the Hanukkah lights.

בָּרוּךְ אַתָּה, יְיָ אֱלֹהֵינוּ, מֶלֶךְ הָעוֹלָם, שֶׁעָשָׂה נִסִּים
לַאֲבוֹתֵינוּ, בַּיָּמִים הָהֵם, בַּזְּמַן הַזֶּה:

Ba-rooch a-ta a-do-nai, el-o-hey-nu me-lech ha-o-lam,
sheh-asa nee-seem la-a-vo-tey-nu ba-ya-meem ha-hem
baz-zman haz-zeh.

Blessed are you, Lord our God, King of the Universe,
who performed miracles for our ancestors in days gone by,
at this season of the year.

## Parent's Summary • Hanukkah

Many Jewish holidays commemorate events invested with historical and religious meaning. The story of Hanukkah is the struggle for religious freedom. Over a thousand years ago, the foreign rulers of the Israelites decreed that the Jews were to bow down to the statue of their leader, Antiochus. But the Jews were forbidden by the law God gave them to bow to statues or idols. Inspired by Mattathias and led by his son, Judah, a small group of Jews called Maccabees (meaning "hammer") rebelled. The Maccabees risked their lives to live according to Jewish law and to prevent the desecration of their sacred Temple.

Although the Maccabees won, the Temple in Jerusalem, the Jews' holy place, was destroyed. The Jews cleaned and repaired the Temple and rededicated it to God by rekindling the *menorah,* the candelabrum symbolizing the eternal covenant between God and the Jewish people and the continuity of tradition through the generations. There was only enough olive oil to fuel the menorah for one night, and it would have taken eight days to make more oil. The Legend of the miracle of Hanukkah says that the one day supply of oil burned until more could be made to keep the flame constantly lit.

Hanukkah is celebrated in the home on the 25th day of the Jewish month of Kislev. Hanukkah is not a major festival in the Jewish liturgical calendar, but it has taken on importance in this country because of its proximity to Christmas. It is traditional to give small gifts to children on each night. The party atmosphere is enhanced with songs and games such as *dreydel,* a spinning top. Yet the religious celebration—the lighting of the candles with accompanying prayers—must come before the party.

## Lesson 4

# Passover

## Introduction

Passover (*Pesach*) is one of the greatest stories of religious freedom ever told. Western civilization has commemorated the story of the Exodus for thousands of generations. Passover relives the Exodus—the Israelites' struggle from slavery to freedom and their covenant with God at Mount Sinai. The quest for religious freedom, for the right to be a Jew, is an ongoing struggle, and the Jewish people commit themselves anew to it each Passover.

Passover and Easter come at roughly the same time every spring. Some of the rituals and symbols of the two celebrations overlap: the Seder table, the egg, the wine and the wafer-like matzo. The Jewish heritage of Jesus is especially apparent at this time. Easter and Passover also have been associated historically in some areas with conflict between Jews and Christians. One point at issue was the so-called "deicide" charge, which held the Jews are forever responsible for the crucifixion of Jesus. In addition, legends grew up suggesting that Jews killed Christians at Easter and used their blood to make matzo. Vatican II repudiated the "deicide" charge and the "blood libel" legends and emphasized God's continuing love for the Jewish people. Passover and Easter are good times to discuss the relationships between Christians and Jews.

## Background

Passover is observed in the spring for seven or eight days (traditions vary) and is one of the three harvest/pilgrimage festivals in the Jewish calendar. Passover is not only a celebration of spring but a celebration of the story of Exodus—the passing of the Israelites from slavery in Egypt to freedom and deliverance. Passover also honors God's gift at Mt. Sinai of the Ten Commandments, around which the Jewish community was formed and continues to evolve.

Passover is a family event, celebrated in the home with every member and guest taking part. For weeks, the house is prepared with a massive spring cleaning. The preparations set apart the time and place as holy. The Seder is held on the first night of Passover and is sometimes repeated on the second night. At the Seder the story of Exodus is experienced by reading from a book called the *Haggadah*. Jews must put themselves in the story, as if they were slaves in Egypt struggling for freedom, so that the story of the Exodus is experienced, not merely retold.

The story begins with a pharaoh who forgets Joseph (of the coat of many colors), who had helped the Egyptians through famine. This pharaoh fears the growing number of Jews in Egypt and orders the murder of Jewish male babies and the enslavement of all Jews. Miriam saves her baby brother Moses by placing him in a basket in the bullrushes. The baby Moses is later found and raised by an Egyptian princess. God chooses Moses to speak to the Egyptian pharaoh on behalf of the Israelites. God sends plagues on the Egyptians until they agree to let the Jews go. The last of the plagues, the death of the first-born males, passes over the Jewish houses marked by the blood of a lamb.

The parting of the sea for the Israelites, the wandering in the desert and God's gift of manna are also part of the story. Central to Exodus is the gift of the Ten Commandments at Mt. Sinai. This gift formed the covenant between the Jewish people and God and provided the basis for the formation of a community dedicated to justice and piety.

The Seder is a combination of ritual, tradition, prayer and celebratory meal. The Haggadah guides the celebrants through the ritual, prayers, stories and songs of the Seder, often in a question and answer format. The Haggadah is read aloud, sometimes with the participants reading in unison and often with each person at the seder table taking a turn.

A favorite part of the seder is the Four Questions asked by the youngest person at the table and answered by the oldest. The well-known first question, "Why is this night different from all other nights?" marks the beginning of the reading from the Haggadah.

The Seder meal is a central part of Jewish liturgy, even though it takes place in the home rather than in the synagogue. The Seder symbols and ritual foods are an important part of the Passover story. There is no leavening (yeast) in any of the food, symbolizing the haste with which the Israelites left Egypt. Flat, cracker-like bread called *matzo* is eaten, and *matzo* meal is used for cooking and baking.

The ritual Seder plate displays the other foods eaten that night: *bitter herbs* (horseradish) to symbolize the bitterness of slavery; *boiled eggs* and *parsley dipped in salt water* to symbolize the green life of spring and the tears of the slaves; *charoses* (chopped apples, nuts, cinnamon and wine) to symbolize the mortar for the bricks the slaves made; the *shank bone of a lamb* to symbolize the lamb's blood the Jews used to mark their houses when the angel of death passed over to take the Egyptian first-born sons.

For centuries, Jews all over the world have ended the Seder by saying, "Next year in Jerusalem." Jerusalem symbolizes Israel, the land of the covenant with God. The desire to return to this land has included the desire to practice Judaism without restriction in a Jewish context. Passover is a holiday honoring the struggle for the freedom to be Jewish.

## Lesson Plan

1. Review "Introducing a Lesson" on pages 5–6. If needed, use the material found there to begin the class.

2. Read the story of Exodus aloud, either from the Hebrew Scriptures or from a *Haggadah*. Talk about what it would be like not to be free. Older children can tell the story together; they can remember it quite well. Let one child start, and then everyone can help to remember and put the pieces together.

3. Discuss how members of the Jewish community celebrate Passover today, particularly the Seder meal.

4. Read the first of the Four Questions, found on the student's Take Home Page. Discuss what it might mean to a small child to recite it in public for the first time. Distribute the Take Home Page to the class and listen to the Four Questions on the audiotape.

5. Taste some Passover foods. *Charoses* commemorates the mortar the Jewish slaves made to cement bricks in Egypt. It is made by mixing finely chopped nuts (pecans or walnuts) with apples, grape juice and cinnamon. *Matzo* is unleavened bread and commemorates the hardship of the Exodus. Horseradish is for the bitterness of slavery. It can be bought in a jar if it is not available fresh. Using the *matzo*, make a sandwich with the charoses and a small amount of horseradish. This is called a Hillel sandwich and is named after a very famous rabbi.

Often, older children will be able to understand the symbolism of the food; they will be able to make connections between the food and the story. It is fun after you have recalled the story together to see how the foods help you remember the story again.

## Additional Plans

1. Attend a Seder in a Jewish home or synagogue.

2. Prepare a Seder jointly with a synagogue or Jewish group.

3. Learn to say the Hebrew word *Dayenu,* and sing along with the song *Dayenu* on the audiotape. *Dayenu* is the only word in the chorus and it means "it would have been enough," referring to each of the wonderful things that God did for the Jewish people.

4. Draw a Jewish family at the Seder table.

## Audiotape

The audiotape for this lesson contains:
The folktune *"Dayenu"* (0:27).
"Planting Song," by Jeff Klepper, arranged by Greg Zelman (1:09).
The traditional Four Passsover Questions (1:27).

## Questions and Answers

*1. Who goes to a Seder?*

The Seder is a family meal. Invitations are often given to friends, neighbors and Jews without family nearby.

*2. Why is food so important during Passover?*

The dietary laws associated with Passover are part of the commemoration of God's delivering the Jewish people from slavery. The ban on leavened food symbolizes the haste with which the Jews had to leave Egypt; they did not even having time to wait for their bread to rise. By sharing in the experience of Exodus, contemporary Jews are connected to a peoplehood that transcends time and place.

*3. Are children forced to eat all of the Passover food?*

Everyone is encouraged to taste everything. However, no one is forced to do so. Babies probably do not get the chance to taste any of the foods.

*4. Can you make a pizza out of matzo meal?*

While you can grind up *matzos* into meal, leavening such as yeast cannot be used. Therefore, it would be very difficult to make a good pizza.

*5. What are the door posts referred to in the story of the lamb's blood marking the Jewish houses?*

The door posts are the entranceway to the house. The entrance way has strong symbolic meaning because by passing in between the posts one steps into a different world. Contemporary Jewish homes often have a special religious object (a *mezzuzah*) on the door posts to separate the home from the secular world.

*6. How young is the youngest child who asks the Four Questions?*

The Four Questions are chanted in Hebrew, and the child who does this part of the Seder must be old enough to have learned how to do this. There is no set age, but often kindergartners have already learned these questions in Hebrew.

*7. Why do some people have grape juice instead of wine at the Seder?*

The Seder participants are required to fill their wine glasses four times during the meal. Since this is unwise for young children, grape juice made especially for Passover is often used for them.

*8. Where do people sit for the Seder?*

Seders are held at the dining table and at whatever extra tables are set up to accommodate the often large crowd. Usually, pillows from around the house and of various sizes are put on the regular chairs at the dining table and people lean on them. In ancient days, chairs and pillows were luxuries that slaves could not afford. The Seder marks freedom by using these luxuries as part of the ritual.

This Seder plate contains the foods that are eaten on the night of Passover: a leg-bone of a lamb; a mixture of chopped apples, nuts, cinnamon and wine called *charoses*; bitter herbs; parsley in salt water; and a boiled egg.

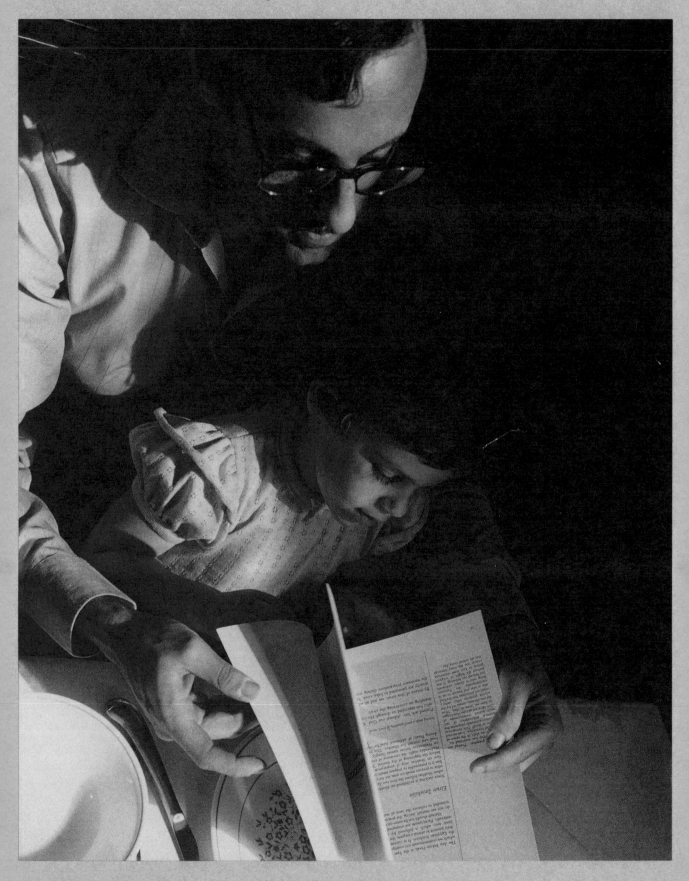

During the Seder meal the family experiences the story of the Jews' escape from the slavery of Egypt. A book called the *Haggadah* contains the prayers, stories and songs of the Seder meal.

Flat bread called *matzo* is eaten during the Seder. *Matzo* is flat because it contains no yeast. It reminds the Jews of the difficulty of the escape from slavery in Egypt and of the hard journey to the Promised Land.

# Passover

At Passover, the Jewish community relives the story of the Exodus. Passover is celebrated at home with a special meal called the Seder. A book called the Haggadah guides the family in the prayers, stories and songs of the Seder. A favorite part of the Seder is the "Four Questions." All of the foods at the meal eaten from the Seder plate help everyone remember the Exodus story.

### The four questions

מַה נִּשְׁתַּנָּה הַלַּיְלָה הַזֶּה מִכָּל הַלֵּילוֹת.

שֶׁבְּכָל הַלֵּילוֹת אָנוּ אוֹכְלִין חָמֵץ וּמַצָּה, הַלַּיְלָה הַזֶּה כֻּלּוֹ מַצָּה.

שֶׁבְּכָל הַלֵּילוֹת אָנוּ אוֹכְלִין שְׁאָר יְרָקוֹת, הַלַּיְלָה הַזֶּה מָרוֹר.

שֶׁבְּכָל הַלֵּילוֹת אֵין אָנוּ מַטְבִּילִין אֲפִילוּ פַּעַם אֶחָת, הַלַּיְלָה הַזֶּה שְׁתֵּי פְעָמִים.

שֶׁבְּכָל הַלֵּילוֹת אָנוּ אוֹכְלִין בֵּין יוֹשְׁבִין וּבֵין מְסֻבִּין, הַלַּיְלָה הַזֶּה כֻּלָּנוּ מְסֻבִּין.

Why is this night different from all other nights?

On all other nights, we may eat either leavened or unleavened bread; on this night, we eat only unleavened bread.

On all other nights, we eat all kinds of herbs; on this night, we eat only bitter herbs. On all other nights, we do not dip (the vegetables) even once; on this night, we have to dip them twice.

On all other nights, we eat either in a sitting or in a reclining position; on this night, we all recline.

## Parent's Summary • Passover

Passover is one of the greatest stories of religious freedom ever told. Western civilization has commemorated the story of the Exodus for thousands of generations. Passover relives the Exodus, the Israelites' struggle from slavery to freedom and their covenant with God at Mount Sinai. The quest for religious freedom, for the right to be a Jew, is an ongoing struggle, and the Jewish people commit themselves anew to it each Passover.

Passover is a family event, celebrated in the home with every member and guest taking part. The various preparations set apart the time and place as holy. On the first night of Passover, the story of Exodus is experienced, not just retold, at the Seder. The Seder is a combination of ritual, tradition, prayer and celebratory meal. The book known as the *Haggadah* guides the celebrants through the ritual, prayers, stories and songs of the Seder, which have been passed down through the generations.

For centuries, Jews all over the world have ended the Seder by saying, "Next year in Jerusalem." Jerusalem symbolizes Israel, the land of the covenant with God. The desire to return to this land has included the desire to practice Judaism without restriction in a Jewish context. The beauty of the Seder is such that it can be admired by all who believe in God. Passover is often seen as a holiday honoring the struggle for religious freedom for all people.

# Lesson 5

# Scripture

## Introduction

The Jewish Bible both overlaps and differs from the Christian Bible. There is no Old or New Testament in Judaism: There are only the Hebrew Scriptures, which many Christians call the Old Testament. The Hebrew Scriptures are called *TaNaKh*, the Hebrew initials for its three sections: Torah, Prophets and Writings. The Torah, composed of the five books of Moses (the first five books of the Bible), is key to understanding the covenant between God and the Jews. It is like a family history. Torah is God's gift to the Jewish people and a Torah scroll itself is a sacred object. Study of the Torah is included in worship. This dedication to scripture is shared by Christians.

After the fall of the Temple (70 CE), the books of the Hebrew Scriptures were formalized. There followed centuries of commentary (Talmud) on scripture and on the meaning of God's commandments. The Talmudic laws—ethics and guides to observances—shaped the Jewish community in many lands and through many generations. In fact, the Talmud influenced the development of Judaism as much as the scriptures did.

## Background

Every copy of the Torah is an exact replica of what has been handed down over the generations. Handwritten entirely in Hebrew on sheets of parchment wound around two poles, the Torah scroll is cherished for its history, religious significance and artistry. The Torah scroll is "dressed" in a heavy decorative covering for its protection and beautification. The posts are often adorned with bells, whose jingle signals that it is time for prayer. Sacred and valuable, the Torah scrolls are kept in the ark of the covenant, which is central to the sanctuary of a synagogue.

It is an honor to hold, touch and read from the Torah. A special pointer, called a *yad*, is used by the reader to help keep his or her place. One must be at least thirteen years of age to read in public from the Torah. Each week, a portion of the Torah is read to the congregation. Prayers are recited before and after the readings to set them apart. During many worship services, a procession carrying the Torah winds through the congregation, whose members reach out to touch or kiss it.

It takes a full year to complete the reading of the Torah during the congregation's weekly gathering. A joyous celebration called Simhat Torah marks the completion of one year of the reading of the Torah and the beginning of another. At Simhat Torah, the Jewish community rejoices in God's gift of the Torah. Holding the Torah, community members dance, sing and wave flags, sometimes all night long. The Torah is a symbol of God's love for the Jewish people, and it is called the community's tree of life.

The study of the Torah is central to the life of the community. Torah study is included in the education of Jewish children who are preparing for acceptance into the adult religious community. Commentary on the Torah and its application to contemporary life has been part of the Jewish community for centuries. The oral tradition that evolved from this commentary defined and refined many of the teachings in the Torah, including those dealing with charity, ethics, business practices, rituals and marriage traditions. This oral tradition, known as Talmud, shaped Judaism through many centuries and many lands, making Judaism a dynamic, evolving faith.

# Lesson Plan

1. Review "Introducing a Lesson" on pages 5–6. If needed, use the material found there to begin the class.

2. Using photos and drawings, talk about the Torah scroll—what it looks like, how it is made, where it is kept, who reads it, when it is read, etc. Talk about how the Torah tells the story of the Jewish people and God. Ask the students to name some of the people in the family history of the Torah. Examples include Adam and Eve, Abraham and Sarah, Noah and Moses. Older children (and adults) may want to try to remember some of the lineage in the order it is presented in the Five Books of Moses.

3. Discuss the holiday called Simhat Torah.
   a. How does the name Simhat Torah (rejoicing in Torah) fit the holiday?
   b. What kinds of activities take place on Simhat Torah?

4. Listen to the traditional Hebrew blessing that is said before the Torah reading. Ask the students about what it makes them think or feel. (It may be recited or chanted by the Jewish teaching partner, or the audiotape may be used.)

# Additional Plans

1. Have a Simhat Torah treat for a sweet year: apples and a sweet (eg., caramel apples).

2. Take a field trip to a synagogue.

3. Older students may compare the table of contents in the Hebrew Scriptures to that of the Christian Bible. Comparing Bibles helps to show that Jews and Christians share scriptures and that Jews do not have the story of Jesus in their Bible. This is part of discovering the similarities and differences between Judaism and Christianity.

# Audiotape

The audiotape for this lesson contains:
The folktunes *"Simhat Torah"* (0:28) and *"Simhas Torah"* (1:07).
The traditional blessing before the Torah reading (1:10).
*"Shechecheyanu,"* by Jeff Klepper (1:00).

# Questions and Answers

## 1. Who hand-writes a Torah scroll?

Each Torah is hand-written in black ink by a scribe who is professionally trained. There are only about one hundred full-time scribes in the world.

## 2. What happens if the scribe makes a mistake writing the Torah?

The Torah must be perfect; a scroll with errors cannot be used. No variations are allowed, so that the tradition and the words are handed down through the generations intact. A knife or pumice stone can remove mistaken letters, except in the word for "God," in which case that sheet of parchment must be discarded.

## 3. How much does a Torah cost?

A Torah is expensive, with costs for the scrolls alone ranging between fifteen and sixty thousand dollars. The coverings and decorations for the Torah increase the cost. The Torah is considered the most important treasure of the community.

## 4. How heavy is a Torah?

A Torah will frequently weigh as much as 20 pounds.

## 5. How long is a Torah scroll if it is rolled out fully?

A Torah scroll is over 21 feet long, but it is not opened this way when it is read in the synagogue. The parchment is kept rolled on the posts and only the portion containing the specific reading is unrolled at any given time.

## 6. Does every Torah say the same thing?

Each Torah says exactly the same thing. The scribe copies it from an existing Torah so that the tradition is handed down intact.

## 7. How long does it take to write a Torah scroll?

It takes more than one thousand hours for a scribe to write a Torah. This means that if the scribe worked a 40 hour week, it would take about 6 months to produce just one Torah scroll.

## 8. Can rabbis get married?

Rabbis can get married and are encouraged to marry and have children. Rabbis are not priests; they are teachers and leaders of the community.

## 9. Does a rabbi have to know Hebrew?

Yes, a rabbi must read and speak Hebrew. The rabbi must lead the Hebrew prayers and be able to read from the Torah. While some synagogues have some of their prayers in English as well as in Hebrew, the Torah is written only in Hebrew.

## 10. Can a woman be a rabbi?

In some branches of Judaism, the tradition that rabbis are male is still upheld. However, in the Reform and Conservative branches of Judaism, it is increasingly common to see women rabbis. At least half of rabbinic students in Reform Judaism are women.

## 11. Does Judaism have priests?

There have been no priests in Judaism since the fall of the Temple in Jerusalem in 70 CE. After that, rabbis became the leaders of communities of Jews.

## 12. When is Simhat Torah?

This holiday is on the 23rd day of the month of Tishri and follows Sukkot (see Lesson One). In the secular calendar, this means that Simhat Torah is in the fall. Simhat Torah celebrates the end of the Torah readings for one year and the beginning of a new cycle of Torah readings.

## 13. What does Simhat Torah mean?

Simhat Torah is Hebrew for "Rejoicing in the Torah."

## 14. How does the Torah begin?

The first word in Genesis is B'reshit, "In the beginning." The last word read in Deuteronomy is "Israel."

The Torah is the first five books of the Bible. Each Torah is handwritten on sheets of parchment and wound around two poles. The Torah scroll is a sacred object for the Jewish people.

A specially trained writer—a scribe—prints the Torah by hand in black ink. It takes more than 1,000 hours for a scribe to write a Torah.

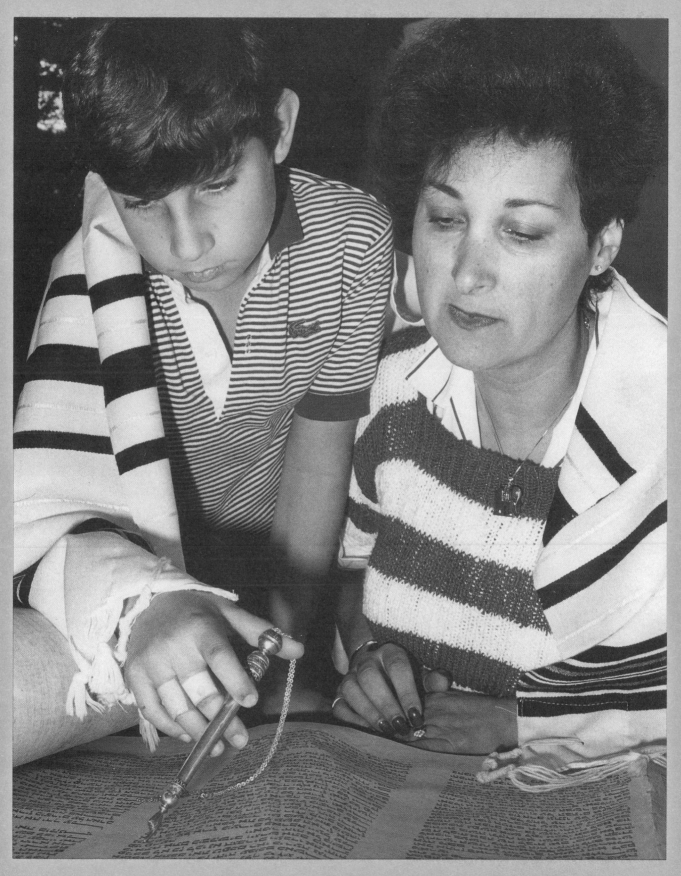

It is an honor to read from the Torah. A special pointer called a *yad* is used by the reader to keep his or her place. One must be at least 13 years old to read form the Torah in the synagogue.

The Torah scrolls are kept covered when they are not being used. The covers are decorated with crowns and pendants, and often the posts are adorned with bells.

# Scripture

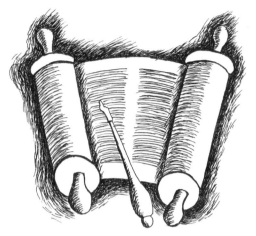

The Torah scroll is a holy object. The books of the Torah are Genesis,
Exodus, Leviticus, Numbers and Deuteronomy. Every week a part of the Torah is read in
the synagogue. The study of the Torah is very important to the life of
the Jewish community.

The Hebrew letters for Torah are:

## Parent's Summary • Scripture

The Jewish Bible both overlaps and differs from the Christian Bible. There is no Old or New Testament in Judaism. There are only the Hebrew Scriptures, which many Christians call the Old Testament. The Torah, the first five books of scripture, is sometimes called the Five Books of Moses and tells the story of God's covenant with the Jews. Torah is God's gift to the Jewish people and a Torah scroll is a sacred object.

It is an honor to hold, touch and read from the Torah scroll. A special pointer, called a *yad*, is used by the reader to help keep his or her place. One must be at least thirteen years of age to read in public from the Torah. Each week, a portion of the Torah is read to the congregation. Prayers are recited before and after the readings to set them apart. The study of the Torah is central to the life of the community. Torah study is included in the education of Jewish children who are preparing for acceptance into the adult religious community.

Commentary on the Torah and its application to contemporary life has been part of the Jewish community for centuries. The oral tradition, or Talmud, defined and refined many biblical teachings including those dealing with charity, ethics, business practices and rituals. This body of oral tradition influenced the development of Judaism as much as the scriptures did.

# Lesson 6

# Prayer and the Sabbath

## Introduction

The prayers, rituals and traditions of the Sabbath are central to Judaism. The Jewish Sabbath begins at sunset on Friday and ends at sunset on Saturday. The Sabbath is a day of peace and rest. It is observed to honor God, who rested on the seventh day of creation. Traditionally, the Sabbath is observed at home and is set apart from daily life in order to keep it holy. It is *mitzvah* (a commandment, a good deed and a blessing) to observe Shabbat, as it is called in Hebrew. Christianity folded some of the elements of the Jewish Sabbath into its celebration of the Lord's Day.

## Background

Preparations for the Sabbath begin during the day on Friday. The family cleans the house and themselves, preparing for the presence of God in the home. Traditionally, the Sabbath candles are lit just before sunset. The light from the candles symbolizes the divine light of creation, peace, faith and remembrance. Prayers of blessing accompany the kindling of the Sabbath lights.

The Sabbath dinner table is set with a white table cloth, a decorative covering for the *challah* (braided bread), fresh flowers and wine glasses. The table shimmers and glows and looks like the Sabbath bride, a beautiful metaphor for God's presence. The wine is blessed with a prayer thanking God for the fruit of the vine. The prayer over the *challah* is offered as if the *challah* were a sacrifice in the ancient Temple and the table were its altar. The bread is broken, and the pieces are shared with the family and guests who form a community for the meal. The meal is the biggest and best of the week, celebrating God's gift of nourishment and life.

The other six days of the week are as bridesmaids leading up to the Sabbath bride, the most important day of the week. On the Sabbath, the participants can glimpse the peace that is salvation. A common Sabbath greeting is *"Shabbat Shalom,"* which means "Sabbath peace." The Sabbath connects Jews to God and to God's creation as described in Genesis. The observance of the Sabbath is so important that according to one legend, if Jews all over the world light the Sabbath candles at the same time, the messiah will come.

## Lesson Plan

1. Review "Introducing a Lesson" on pages 5–6. If needed, use the material found there to begin the class.

2. The first part of this lesson explores how Christians understand their own tradition of prayer.

   a. Brainstorm about why Christians pray (praise, thanks, forgiveness, help, etc.).
   b. Discuss where Christians pray (church, school, home, hospital, cemetery, etc.).
   c. Discuss to whom Christians pray and how (to God, hands folded in prayer position, arms outstretched, standing, kneeling, alone, with others).

3. The second part of this lesson explores how Jews pray.

   a. The "why" is very similar to the reasons Christians pray.
   b. The "where" is also similar, but the home/family rituals are central in Judaism.
   c. "To whom" is also similar (God) and yet different (not to Jesus, or to the Holy Spirit).

Note: Jews do not make the sign of the cross, have rosaries, statues of Jesus or of anyone else, or hold their hands in any prayer position. Jews do not kneel during prayer. However, some Jews may sway or rock gently back and forth during prayers.

4. Experience of Sabbath worship. (Encourage Jewish partners to share home rituals and objects. Otherwise, use the resources in this book.)

   a. Show photos of the Sabbath candles, wine glasses and challah.
   b. Listen to the Hebrew prayers on the audiotape that are chanted over each of the above items. Ask the students what these prayers remind them of.
   c. Look at a picture of a Jewish family sitting down to Sabbath dinner. Identify the objects that are part of the Sabbath ritual.

5. Read and discuss the poem *"Havdalah,"* by Carol Adler. *Havdalah* means separation and is the name for the brief ceremony that concludes the Sabbath. At the Havdalah ritual a thick, multi-wicked candle is lit and is held in the hand so that you can see the light reflected off the fingernails. The participants each have a glass of wine accompanied by blessings of thanksgiving. A box of sweet smelling spices adds to the enjoyment of the ceremony; the aroma is meant to symbolize the joy of the Sabbath and carry the spirit of the Sabbath into the rest of the week.

## Havdalah
*by Carol Adler*

"A good week," we sing
at the end of Shabbat.

A week as bright as
candlelight, as
sweet as spice
and sweeter than wine!

"A good week!" we sing
as we light the candles
sniff the spice box
and lifting the wine cup
take a sip.
Can you see the light
dancing on your fingertips?
Can you feel inside
another week
ready to begin?

# Audiotape

The audiotape for this lesson contains:
The folksong "*L'Cha Dodi*," arranged by Greg Zelman (2:35).
"*Shalom Rov*," by Ben Steinberg (2:28).
"*Sim Shalom*," by M. Isaacson (3:59).
"*Hashkiveynu*," by Max Janowski (4:22).
The traditional candle blessing (0:18).
The traditional wine and *challah* blessing (2:00).

# Questions and Answers

## 1. Do Jews wear special clothes when praying?

Jewish people enjoy dressing up for the Sabbath. Some cover their heads and wear a prayer shawl for Sabbath prayers. More traditional Jewish males may wrap items known as "phylacteries" (small boxes containing special prayers) around their forearms and forehead.

## 2. Do Jewish children have parochial schools where they pray?

There are "parochial" schools for Jewish children. They are called day schools. In addition, children who attend public schools go after school and on Sunday to religious education classes.

## 3. When do the Sabbath candles get blown out?

The Sabbath candles do not get blown out. They are allowed to burn until there is nothing left. Only the *Havdalah* candle is extinguished by the participants to show the end of the sacred time of the Sabbath.

## 4. What do Jews think about Jesus?

While some Jews may consider Jesus a teacher and leader, there is generally little said about Jesus at all. Jewish people do not believe that Jesus is the messiah. Nor is the Trinity a Jewish concept. God is described by metaphor and attributes and can be referred to simply as *HaShem*, which translated means "the name."

## 5. Do Jews celebrate Christmas or Easter?

Christmas and Easter center on Jesus and are not part of Judaism. While Jews appreciate the beauty of Christmas and the solemnity of Easter for their Christian neighbors, these holidays do not appear in the Jewish liturgical calendar.

## 6. What activities do Jews have on the Sabbath?

The Sabbath is set aside to keep it holy. Jews are expected to reflect this holiness by rest, contemplation and the study of Judaism. The goal is to honor God's creation by resting on the seventh day as God did. Sabbath activities center around the family and the synagogue.

## 7. *Are there special foods that go along with the Sabbath?*

The wine and *challah* (braided bread) celebrating the Sabbath are part of its liturgy and are followed by a large joyous meal. Sharing a meal together is a very basic part of the life of the Jewish community. There are some dietary laws that are observed. Laws for keeping kosher prohibit eating anything made from pork or shellfish. Mixing meat with dairy products is also prohibited. Kosher restrictions are outlined in the Hebrew Scriptures and in other texts. They are kept to varying degrees by the different branches of modern-day Judaism.

## 8. *What happens at the end of the Sabbath?*

A brief ceremony called *Havdalah,* which means "separation," marks the end of the sacred time of the Sabbath. The Havdalah participants light a special candle and say prayers of thanksgiving. The aroma from a box of spices ends the Sabbath. The smells, sounds and sights of Havdalah carry the spirit and peace of the Sabbath into the rest of the week.

The Sabbath dinner table is prepared with candles, flowers, wine glasses and braided bread called *challah*. After the candles are lit, the wine and bread are blessed and shared.

When the Sabbath ends on Saturday, a special braided candle is lit. A special box of spices is also used. The pleasant smell of the spices reminds the family of the joy of the Sabbath throughout the week.

# Prayer and the Sabbath

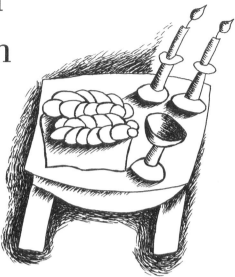

The Sabbath is the most beautiful day of the week for Jews. It begins at sunset on Friday and ends at sunset on Saturday. On Friday evening, Jewish families have a special Sabbath dinner with special blessing prayers for the candles, bread and wine. The Sabbath is a holy day. It honors God and all that God created, and remembers that God rested on the seventh day of creation.

### Blessing for Lighting the Sabbath Candles

בָּרוּךְ אַתָּה, יְיָ אֱלֹהֵינוּ, מֶלֶךְ הָעוֹלָם, אֲשֶׁר קִדְּשָׁנוּ בְּמִצְוֹתָיו וְצִוָּנוּ
לְהַדְלִיק נֵר שֶׁל שַׁבָּת.

Ba-rooch a-ta a-do-nai, el-o-hey-nu me-lech ha-o-lam

Blessed are you, Lord our God, King of the Universe,
[who has blessed us with the commandments, and commanded us to light the Sabbath lights.]

### Blessing for the Wine

בָּרוּךְ אַתָּה, יְיָ אֱלֹהֵינוּ, מֶלֶךְ הָעוֹלָם, בּוֹרֵא פְּרִי הַגָּפֶן.

Ba-rooch a-ta a-do-nai, el-o-hey-nu me-lech ha-o-lam,
bo-rei p're ha-ga-fen.
Blessed are you, Lord our God, Kind of the Universe, who creates the fruit of the vine.

### Blessing for the Bread

בָּרוּךְ אַתָּה, יְיָ אֱלֹהֵינוּ, מֶלֶךְ הָעוֹלָם,
הַמּוֹצִיא לֶחֶם מִן הָאָרֶץ.

Ba-rooch a-ta a-do-nai, el-o-hey-nu me-lech ha-o-lam,
ha-motzi lech-em min ha-artez.

Blessed are you, Lord our God, King of the Universe, who brings forth bread from the earth.

## Parent's Summary • Prayer and the Sabbath

The prayers, rituals and traditions of the Sabbath are central to Judaism. The Jewish Sabbath begins at sunset on Friday and ends at sunset on Saturday. The Sabbath is set apart from daily life in order to keep it holy. It honors the story of creation in Genesis when God rested on the seventh day of creating the world.

The Sabbath dinner table is set with a white table cloth, a decorative covering for the *challah* (braided bread), fresh flowers and wine glasses. The table shimmers and glows and looks like a Sabbath bride, a beautiful metaphor for God's presence. The wine is blessed with a prayer thanking God for the fruit of the vine. The prayer over the *challah* is offered as if the *challah* were a sacrifice in the ancient Temple and the table were its altar.

The other six days of the week are as bridesmaids leading up to the Sabbath bride, the most important day of the week. On the Sabbath the participants can glimpse the peace that is salvation. A common greeting on the Sabbath is *"Shabbat Shalom,"* which means "Sabbath peace." The celebration of the Sabbath connects Jews to God and to God's creation as described in Genesis. The observance of the Sabbath is so important that according to one legend, if Jews all over the world light the Sabbath candles at the same time, the messiah will come.

# Lesson 7

# Gathering in the Synagogue

## Introduction

In developing their synagogues, Jews created many of the precedents for combining tradition, ritual, sacred space and prayer in a house of worship. History, community and Torah intersect in this sacred space. Every synagogue has certain traditional elements that have been part of the faith for hundreds of generations, yet each synagogue also reflects the taste and character of its congregation in its architecture, seating arrangements, musicians' accommodations and many other details. Therefore, what one experiences in the synagogue is not only a biblical people but an evolving tradition of faith.

The individual Jew learns the traditions, rituals and prayers of the faith, but it is the communal context that gives the religion much of its power. The interplay of the individual and the community is particularly visible in the celebration of the *bar mitzvah* or the *bat mitzvah*, in which a child is accepted into the adult congregation. This reaffirming celebration renews the commitment of the community while it shapes the individual. The centuries-old ritual links the community to a Jewish peoplehood that transcends time and place.

## Background

The Jewish community prays together in the synagogue, a word meaning "meeting place of the covenantal people." Some synagogues are called temples, the reference being to the ancient Temple in Jerusalem. The Temple was built around the "holy of holies," where the ark of the covenant was kept. Built on the Temple Mount of Jerusalem, the Temple was the holy place of Judaism and is still revered today.

The Temple was destroyed in 586 BCE and again in 70 CE. During the first exile, synagogues developed as meeting places and were connected with worship, religious study and debate. After the fall of the second Temple, the synagogue became the focus of Judaism and continues to be the house of worship for contemporary Jewish communities.

The rituals, sacrifices and priests of the Temple were replaced by prayers and traditions in the synagogue and home. The synagogue became a place of prayer, study and communal gathering. Through the centuries, a large body of commentary on the Torah was created by rabbis (teachers). This commentary formed an oral tradition—Talmud—whose laws, traditions, ethics and ritual guides shaped Judaism as much as the Torah did. Modern Jews retain their connection with the Hebrew Scriptures but are also the heirs of this later rabbinic tradition.

The scrolls of the Torah became the center of worship and of the synagogue. The scrolls are kept in the ark of the covenant, which remains closed when the Torah is not in use. Over the ark is a continuously burning light, the *Ne'er Tamid* ("Eternal Flame"), which symbolizes the eternal covenant of God with the Jewish people. The ark and the Eternal Flame are often elevated so that the congregation can see them and be part of the tradition.

The congregants usually sit during the service, but they stand in respect when the ark is opened. In some synagogues congregants, particularly the men, wear caps covering their heads and prayer shawls during worship as an additional sign of respect. In more traditional synagogues, men may wear phylacteries (small boxes containing special prayers) on their forearms and forehead. Only an honored few are called up to the bima (podium) at any one time to read from the Torah. The prayer book everyone uses draws on biblical and rabbinic writings.

The worship service is divided into four parts. The first part praises God, while the second speaks of God's love and of how the community must respond in covenant. The third section asks for God's blessings and the fourth is a time for each person to pray privately to God. In addition, many worship services include a reading from the Torah.

In Judaism, worship begins with praise, blessings and a call to worship with phrases such as "Blessed are You, Lord our God," and "Praised be You, Almighty God." This is a tradition that has been carried over into Christianity. The sacred language of Judaism is Hebrew, and many prayers continue to be taught to Jewish children in Hebrew and are quickly recalled when the prayer is announced. The prayer called the Sh'ma is often called the watchword of the Jewish religion. This prayer calls upon Jews to declare God's eternal and supreme name and to renew their covenant with God through demonstrations of love and respect. The Sh'ma includes verses from, among other scriptural sources, Deuteronomy 6:4-9 and 11:13-21, and is best known by its first verse, "Hear, O Israel: The Lord is our God, the Lord is One!" (Deuteronomy 6:4)

The rituals of bar mitzvah (for young men) and bat mitzvah (for young women) celebrate the entrance of children into the adult religious community. Through these rituals, the community passes on to yet another generation the revered traditions, prayers and Torah. The study of Hebrew, history, holidays, prayers and especially Torah is required for bar/bat mitzvah. Other, more particular requirements vary within the branches of Judaism. The bar/bat mitzvah has traditionally been the first time a person reads from the Torah in front of the congregation. The Torah is handed from members of the oldest generation to the child in front of the congregation, symbolizing the continuity of the faith, the community and the individual's commitment. In addition, the child must make a speech demonstrating that lessons have been learned and that preparations have been made to accept individual responsibility within the community. The bar/bat mitzvah is but one example of how the dynamics of individual and communal life are renewed in the context of the synagogue.

## Lesson Plan

1. Review "Introducing a Lesson" on pages 5–6. If needed, use the materials found there to begin the class.

2. Using the photographs in this book, explore the synagogue. Ask questions like the following: What is it? What does it look like? What do you see that reminds you of a Christian church? What things are different? Note the important features: scrolls, bima, Ark.

3. Discuss the Sh'ma. Follow the text of the Sh'ma on the Take Home Page as the students listen to versions of it from the audiotape chanted in Hebrew. Ask questions similar to the following: Does it remind you of other languages you have heard? What effect does the chanting have on you? What does it mean to the Jewish people? What are some of the central prayers of Christianity? How are these prayers and the Sh'ma similar? How are they different?

4. Discuss a *bar mitzvah* or a *bat mitzvah* that the students may have seen on television or at the movies or heard about from friends. Discuss its importance for young Jewish people.

5. If a Jewish partner is available, ask for a description from a personal point of view of the role of the *bar mitzvah* and *bat mitzvah* in Jewish life.

## Additional Plans

1. Discuss the following poem.

### "Poem Without an End"
*by Yehuda Amichai*

Inside the brand-new museum
there's an old synagogue.
Inside the synagogue
is me.
Inside me
my heart.
Inside my heart
a museum.
Inside the museum
a synagogue,
inside it
me,
inside me
my heart,
inside my heart a museum.

2. Arrange to visit a synagogue either for a tour and introduction or for a service.

3. Examine a Jewish prayer book to see the Hebrew text and to read some of the English prayers. A Jewish partner can read some of the Hebrew and point out the English translation.

4. Write prayers that begin with praise of God.

## Audiotape

The audiotape for this lesson includes:
The *Bar'chu,* arranged by B. Siegel (1:07)
The *Bar'chu,* arranged by Max Janowski (0:33).
The *Bar'chu,* for use on high holidays, arranged by Max Janowski (0:38).
The *Sh'ma,* arranged by Pik (1:03).
The *Sh'ma,* arranged by Max Janowski (0:41).
The *Sh'ma,* for use on high holidays, arranged by Greg Zelman (0:54).

# Questions and Answers

*1. How long is a Jewish worship service?*

The service varies with the occasion and sometimes with the branch of Judaism. A Sabbath service can last anywhere from one to three hours.

*2. Why don't Christians use any Hebrew in their worship services?*

Christianity developed using different translations of the Bible from the Greek, and Latin became the language of the culture of much of Christianity and of worship. However, there are a few Hebrew words remaining in the Christian liturgy: amen, hosanna and alleluia.

*3. Where is the altar for the sacrifices described in the Hebrew Scriptures?*

There is no altar in synagogues because there are no sacrifices of grains, fruits or animals. Those sacrifices were made by the priests in the Temple of Jerusalem and at no other time or place. The rabbis replaced these practices with prayer.

*4. What kinds of things do Jews do to remember the Temple in Jerusalem?*

At every Jewish wedding, the bridegroom crushes a glass with his foot. The breaking of the glass symbolizes the destruction of the second Temple in Jerusalem. It is a reminder of the faith that has carried Jews through past generations and that will continue to carry them into the future.

*5. When do Jewish children learn Hebrew?*

Some Jewish children go to Jewish day schools and learn Hebrew every day. Most go after school and on Sundays and begin formal studies in Hebrew around the fourth grade.

*6. Why is a* bar mitzvah *or a* bat mitzvah *like a big party?*

Traditionally, the community is invited to celebrate the *bar mitzvah* or *bat mitzvah* with the family after the worship service, usually held on a Saturday (Sabbath) morning. The *bar mitzvah* or *bat mitzvah* marks an important event in the life of the community because it sees its tradition being handed down to the next generation. Gifts are often given to the child on this occasion.

*7. Do all Jews pray in Hebrew?*

Hebrew is the sacred language of Judaism. However, the issue of how much Hebrew to continue using, and what kind of translation is acceptable, is debated in many branches of Judaism.

In each synagogue is an ark containing the covered Torah scrolls.

This Jewish boy is reading to the congregation from the Torah during his *Bar Mitzvah*. Jewish girls also read from the Torah during their *Bat Mitzvah*.

Here a rabbi presides at a Jewish wedding ceremony in a synagogue.

# Gathering in the Synagogue

The synagogue is a place of prayer, study and gathering for the Jewish community. Some Jews call their synagogue a temple. The Torah scrolls are kept in the Ark. The study of the Torah is very important to the life of the Jewish community. The celebration of the *bar mitzvah* for boys and the *bat mitzvah* for girls marks the entry of young people into the adult congregation. At this time, the young person may have the honor of reading from the Torah in the synagogue.

The Call to Prayer: The *Bar'chu.*
Leader:

בָּרְכוּ אֶת־יְיָ הַמְבֹרָךְ!

Ba-re-chu et A-do-nai ha-me-vo-rach.
Praise the Lord, to whom all praise is due.
All:

בָּרוּךְ יְיָ הַמְבֹרָךְ לְעוֹלָם וָעֶד!

Ba-rook A-do-nai ha-me-vo-rach le-o-lam va-ed.
Praised be the Lord to whom all praise is due for ever and ever.

The prayer called the *Sh'ma.*
All:

שְׁמַע יִשְׂרָאֵל: יְיָ אֱלֹהֵינוּ, יְיָ אֶחָד!

She-ma Yis-ra-eil: A-do-nai e-lo-hey-nu A-do-nai E-chad!
Hear, O Israel: The Lord is our God, the Lord is One!
All:

בָּרוּךְ שֵׁם כְּבוֹד מַלְכוּתוֹ לְעוֹלָם וָעֶד!

Ba-rook sheim ke-vod mal-chu-to le-o-lam va-ed!
Blessed is your glorious kingdom for ever and ever!

## Parent's Summary • Gathering in the Synagogue

In developing their synagogues, Jews created many of the precedents for combining tradition, ritual, sacred space and prayer in a house of worship. History, community and Torah intersect in this sacred space. Every synagogue has certain traditional elements that have been part of the faith for hundreds of generations, yet each synagogue also reflects the taste and character of its congregation in its architecture, seating arrangements, musicians' accommodations and many other details. Therefore, what one experiences in the synagogue is not only a biblical people but an evolving tradition of faith.

The rituals, sacrifices and priests of the biblical Temple were replaced by prayers and traditions in the synagogue and home. The synagogue became a place of prayer, study and communal gathering. The Hebrew Scriptures, the Torah, were central to synagogues everywhere. Through the centuries, a large body of commentary on the Torah was created by rabbis (teachers). This commentary formed an oral tradition, Talmud, whose laws, traditions, ethics and ritual guides shaped Judaism as much as the Torah did.

Individual Jews learn the traditions, rituals and prayers of the faith, but it is the communal context that gives the religion much of its power. The interplay of individual and community is particularly visible in the celebration of the *bar mitzvah* and the *bat mitzvah*, in which a young person is accepted into the adult congregation. This reaffirming celebration renews the commitment of the community while it shapes the individual. This centuries-old ritual links the community to a Jewish peoplehood that transcends time and place.

# Glossary

**Note on pronunciation:** The English equivalents of Hebrew words are approximations. You may see varying spellings. A major reason for discrepancies between Hebrew and English is the presence of sounds in the Hebrew alphabet that have no English equivalent. It is recommended that where one sees a "ch" that it generally be pronounced as an "h." There are variations in pronunciation within Judaism itself. The pronunciation in this book is Sephardic, which means that the "th" sound is pronounced as "t" (eg., Kethuvim = Ket-oo-vim). Also, a preferred ending of many words will be "t" rather than "s" (eg., bat mitzvah rather than bas mitzvah).

**Ark:** a cabinet that houses the Torah scrolls, often built into the wall of the synagogue. The ark is the central focus of the synagogue and symbolizes the original Ark of the Covenant.

**B.C.E.:** abbreviation for the phrase Before the Christian Era. Jews use this terminology rather than B.C. ("before Christ"), which is not a frame of reference in Judaism.

**Bar'chu:** a prayer that is also in itself a call to community prayer.

**Bar mitzvah:** the celebration marking a Jewish boy's attaining adult status in the congregation. It is usually celebrated at age thirteen and requires the boy to read from the Torah for the congregation.

**Bat mitzvah:** the celebration marking a Jewish girl's attaining adult status in the congregation. It is celebrated at age twelve or thirteen and requires the girl to read from the Torah for the congregation in Reform, Reconstructionist, and some Conservative Jewish synagogues.

**Bima:** from the Hebrew meaning "high place," the bima is usually a raised area from which the worship service is led.

**B'reshit:** in Hebrew this means "In the beginning," and is the opening of the Book of Genesis.

**C.E.:** abbreviation for Common Era. Jews use this terminology rather than A.D. ("*Anno domini*—in the year of the Lord"), which is not a frame of reference in Judaism.

**Challah:** special braided bread for use on the Sabbath.

**Charoses:** a combination of chopped apples, nuts, cinnamon and wine. It is eaten at Passover and symbolizes the mortar of the bricks the slaves made.

**Conservative Judaism:** a branch of Judaism which blends tradition with modernization and stresses the conservation of tradition.

**Dayenu:** a sixth-century song of joy and thanksgiving sung during the Passover Seder meal. In Hebrew the word means "that would have been enough" and refers to each of God's miracles while bringing the Israelites out of Egypt to Mount Sinai and then into the Promised Land.

**Days of Awe:** the ten days from Rosh Hashanah (New Year) to Yom Kippur (Day of Atonement).

**Dreydel:** a spinning top, traditionally played with on Hanukkah.

The Four Questions: The four prescribed questions are part of the liturgy of the Passover Seder meal. They define the sacred aspects of the Seder for the Jews and encourage the retelling of the story of the Israelites' flight from Egypt. Since the Middle Ages, the youngest family member asks the questions in Hebrew and the oldest member gives the traditional answers. In this way the tradition and ritual are passed on to new generations.

Gelt: money given as a gift at Hanukkah.

Hagaddah: the book that gives the order of the service at Passover.

Hanukkah: Festival of Lights celebrating the rededication of the ancient Temple in Jerusalem.

HaShem: in Hebrew, the word means "the name" and refers to God. The name of God is sacred and is not said aloud or written.

Hassidim: a small group within Judaism that adheres to tradition and is often characterized by a modest style of dress not unlike the Amish.

Havdalah: the brief ceremony closing the Sabbath and beginning the week. The literal meaning is "separation."

Hebrew Scriptures: the Jewish Bible. See *TaNaKh*.

Holocaust: also known as *Shoah*, the Holocaust refers to the historical events of World War II when 6 million Jews—one third of the world's Jews—were systematically killed by the Nazi regime.

Kol Nidre: solemn music played on the evening of Yom Kippur.

Kosher: refers to the dietary laws of Judaism.

Latkes: potato pancakes traditionally linked with Hanukkah.

Maccabees: the Hanukkah story is told in the Book of Maccabees. Maccabee means "hammer" in Hebrew and refers to a small group of Jews, led by Judah Maccabee, who rebelled against foreign domination and religious oppression in the second century B.C.E.

Matzoh: unleavened bread eaten during Passover.

 Menorah: the seven-branched candelabrum in the synagogue. The term is often used specifically to refer to the eight-branched candelabrum used at Hanukkah.

Mezzuzah: a small casing containing a piece of parchment that is inscribed with the biblical commandment to write God's words on the doorpost of one's house (Deuteronomy 6:9). Traditionally, the mezzuzah is fixed to the doorpost and is understood as an affirmation of the sanctity of the Jewish home.

Mitzvah: a good deed, a blessing, a commandment.

 Mogen David: in Hebrew the term means "Shield of David," and refers to the six-pointed star. Since the Middle ages, the Jewish star has been a symbol of the Jewish people.

 Ne'er tamid: the Eternal Light symbolizing the covenant between God and the Jewish people. It is continuously lit and is placed in front of the ark in the synagogue.

Nostra Aetate: Latin title of the document issued in 1965 by the Second Vatican Council. It is the Catholic church's declaration on its relation to non-Christian religions.

**Orthodox Judaism:** a branch of Judaism that emphasizes tradition.

**Pesach:** Passover, the spring harvest/pilgrimage holiday and the celebration of the story of Exodus.

**Phylacteries:** also known as *"tefillin,"* phylacteries are a pair of black leather boxes containing four biblical passages (Exodus 13:1-10; 11-16; Deuteronomy 6:4-9; 11:13-21). During morning prayer, the boxes are bound with leather straps to the hand and forehead, fulfilling biblical commandments.

**Rabbi:** the leader of the Jewish congregation. The word means "teacher."

**Reconstructionist Judaism:** a branch of Judaism that originated from Conservative Judaism but emphasizes certain modern themes, particularly the importance of the Jewish peoplehood.

**Reform Judaism:** a branch of Judaism that has led the movement to modernize the religion.

**Rosh Hashanah:** the Jewish new year. The literal meaning is "Head of the Year."

**Seder:** the Passover meal. The literal meaning is "table."

**Shabbat:** the Sabbath, which begins at sunset on Friday and continues until sunset on Saturday.

**Shabbat Shalom:** Sabbath peace, a common greeting on the Sabbath.

**Shammas:** the extra candle on the Hanukkah menorah used to light the other candles.

**Shavuot:** the summer harvest/pilgrimage festival associated with Moses receiving the Ten Commandments.

**Sh'ma:** the prayer that is the watchword of the Jewish faith: "Hear, O Israel, the Lord our God, the Lord is One."

**Shofar:** the ram's horn blown to call the Jewish people to prayer. It is associated with Rosh Hashanah.

**Shtetl:** this term refers to the European ghettos in which Jews lived until modern times.

**Simhat Torah:** literally, "Rejoicing in the Torah," it is the celebration each year of ending the reading of the Torah and beginning it anew.

**Sukkah:** a temporary dwelling of four sides and a slat roof. Built during the celebration of Sukkot, the sukkah brings Jews closer to the biblical times when they were in the fields for the harvest.

**Sukkot:** the fall harvest/pilgrimage festival giving thanks for God's bounty. The literal meaning is "Festival of Booths."

**Synagogue:** the Jewish house of worship.

**Talmud:** rabbinic commentary on the Hebrew Scriptures, sometimes referred to as the oral tradition.

**TaNaKh:** the Hebrew Scriptures. The letters stand for its three sections: Torah, the Five Books of Moses (first five books of Scripture); Nevi'im, the Prophets; and Kethuvim, the Writings.

**Torah:** the first five books of the Bible, sometimes referred to as the Five Books of Moses. The term is often used to cover all of the Hebrew Scriptures and sometimes the extensive commentary on the Torah.

Yom Kippur: one of the High Holy Days, along with Rosh Hashanah. Also known as the Day of Atonement, it is a fast day at the end of the Ten Days of Awe, which begin with the Jewish New Year, Rosh Hashanah.

# Resources

There are many wonderful books for children and adults and a wide range of audio-visual materials available. Only a few are noted here along with a recommendation to study the catalogs of the publication houses listed below. You might first turn to your local public library. Libraries often have cooperative lending catalogs, so be sure to ask. Also, do not hesitate to investigate your local video store's catalog.

In large and small towns, the local Jewish community may be able to help you. The first places to inquire are the local Jewish Federation of Philanthropies and the Board/Bureau of Jewish Education. Large synagogues also have libraries and gift shops and are generally willing to help.

Adler, David A. *A Picture Book of Hanukkah.* Illustrated by Linda Heller. New York: Holiday House, 1982.

Bloch, Chana, and Mitchell, Stephen, eds. *The Selected Poetry of Yehuda Amichai.* New York: Harper & Row, 1986.

Brinn, Ruth Esrig. *More Let's Celebrate.* Illustrated by Katherine Janus Kahn. Kar-ben Copies, Inc., 1984.

Cone, Molly. *Stories of Jewish Symbols.* Design and illustrations by Siegmund Forst. New York: Bloch Publishing Co., 1963.

Efron, Benjamin. *Pathways Through the Prayerbook.* Prayer translation by Rabbi Samuel M. Silver. Illustrated by Uri Shulevitz. New York: Ktav Publishing House, Inc., 1962.

Einstein, Stephen, and Kukoff, Lydia. *Every Person's Guide to Judaism.* New York: UAHC Press, 1989.

Freeman, Grace R. and Sugarman, Joan G. *Inside the Synagogue.* second edition. Photography by Justin E. Kerr & others. Illustrations by Judith Oren. New York: Union of American Hebrew Congregations, 1965.

Greenberg, Judith, and Carey, Helen. *Jewish Holidays: A First Book.* New York: Franklin Watts, 1984. (For younger children.)

Groner, Judye, and Wikler, Madeline. *All About Hanukkah.* Rockville MD: Kar-Ben Copies, Inc., 1988.

Ganz, Yaffa. *Follow the Moon: A Journey Through the Jewish Year.* Illustrated by Harvey Klineman. Jerusalem: Feldheim Publishers, Ltd., 1984.

*A Hanukah Sing-Along for Kids.* Southgate Distribution, 1988. 316 Southgate Court, Brentwood, Tennessee 37027.

The Klezmer Conservatory Band. *Oy Chanukah!* Rounder Records Corporation, 1986. One Camp Street, Cambridge, Massachusetts 02140. (Rounder C3102) (For grade 4 and older.)
Livingston, Myra Cohen, ed. *Poems for Jewish Holidays.* Illustrated by Lloyd Bloom. New York: Holiday House, 1986. (For younger children.)

Pasochoff, Naomi. *Basic Judaism for Young People: Torah.* New Jersey: Behrman House, Inc., 1986.

Rossel, Seymour. *When Jews Pray.* The Jewish Value Series. With Eugene R. Borowitz, Hyman Chanover. New York: Beerman House, Inc., 1973.

Shapiro, Mark Dov. *Gates of Shabbat: A Guide for Observing Shabbat.* Illustrated by Neil Waldman. New York: Central Conference of American Rabbis, 1991.

Shermis, Michael, and Zannoni, Arthur E., eds. *Introduction to Jewish-Christian Relations.* Mahwah, NJ: Paulist Press, 1991.

Steinkoler, Ronnie. *A Jewish Cookbook for Children.* Illustrated by Sonja Glassman. New York: Julian Messner.

Syme, Daniel B. The Jewish Home: A Guide for Jewish Living. New York: UAHC Press, 1988.

## Resources from Liturgy Training Publications

Jegen, Carol Francis, and Sherwin, Byron. *Thank God: Prayers of Jews and Christians Together.*

Klenicki, Leon, and Fisher, Eugene. *From Desolation to Hope: An Interreligious Holocaust Memorial Service.*

Klenicki, Leon. *The Passover Celebration: A Haggadah for the Seder.*

*Songs for the Seder Meal* an audiotape to accompany *The Passover Celebration*

Pawlikowski, John T., and Wikle, James A. *When Catholics Speak about Jews: Notes for Homilists and Catechists.*

## Publishing and Supply Houses

ARE Publishing, Inc., 3945 South Oneida Street, Denver, CO 80237; phone (800) 346-7779; fax (303) 758-0954.

Behrman House, 235 Watchung Avenue, West Orange, NJ 07052; phone (201) 669-0447; fax (201) 669-9769.

Jewish Publication Society, 1930 Chestnut Street, Philadelphia, PA 19103; phone (215) 564-5925.

Kar-Ben Copies, Inc. 6800 Tilkenwood Lane, Rockville, MD 20852; phone (301) 984-8733.

KTAV Publishing House, Inc. 900 Jefferson Street, Hoboken, NJ 07030; phone (201) 963-9524. Especially good source for supplies such as miniature Torahs, dreydels and other artistic and religious objects.

Torah Aura Productions, 4423 Fruitland Avenue, Los Angeles, CA 90058; phone (800) BE-TORAH; fax (213) 585-0327.

Union of American Hebrew Congregations Press; 838 Fifth Avenue, New York, NY 10021; phone (212) 249-0100.

## Photo Credits

Lesson 1  Interior of Chicago Loop Synagogue, Algiamantas Kezys, photographer, from *Chicago Churches and Synagogues*, published by Loyola University Press, Chicago. Man Drinking Kiddish in Sukkah with Son, Bill Aron, photographer, Tony Stone Images/Chicago, Inc.

Lesson 2  Shofars and ram's horns, from *Let's Learn About Jewish Symbols,* by Joyce Fischman, ©1969 The Union of American Hebrew Congregations, New York. Girl playing shofar, from *Let's Learn About Jewish Symbols,* by Joyce Fischman, ©1969 The Union of American Hebrew Congregations, New York. Two boys blowing shofars, photograph courtesy Torah Aura Productions, Los Angeles.

Lesson 3  Menorah, from *Let's Learn About Jewish Symbols,* by Joyce Fischman, ©1969 The Union of American Hebrew Congregations, New York. Boys playing dreydel at their Talmud Torah school, Annette Rose Kodner, photographer.

Lesson 4  Seder plate, photograph courtesy Torah Aura Productions, Los Angeles. Man and girl reading Haggadah, photograph courtesy Torah Aura Productions, Los Angeles. Boy having Passover Seder with grandfather, Bill Aron, photographer, Tony Stone Images/Chicago, Inc.

Lesson 5  Torah, from *Let's Learn About Jewish Symbols,* by Joyce Fischman, ©1969 The Union of American Hebrew Congregations, New York. Portrait of Orthodox Jew writing, Bill Aron, photographer, Tony Stone Images/Chicago, Inc. Woman and child reading Torah, photograph courtesy Torah Aura Productions, Los Angeles.

Lesson 6  Covered Torah, from *Let's Learn About Jewish Symbols,* by Joyce Fischman, ©1969 The Union of American Hebrew Congregations, New York. Sabbath table seen through window, Bill Aron, photographer, Tony Stone Images/Chicago, Inc. Havdalah set, photograph courtesy Torah Aura Productions, Los Angeles.

Lesson 7  Ark with people in front, photograph courtesy of Torah Aura Productions, Los Angeles. Bar Mitzvah boy reading from Torah, Bill Aron, photographer, Tony Stone Images/Chicago, Inc. Traditional Jewish Wedding at Liberal Synagogue, David Austen, photographer, Tony Stone Images/Chicago, Inc.

## Poem Credits

"Poem Without an End," from *The Selected Poetry of Yehuda Amichai,* by Yehuda Amichai. Edited and translated by Chana Bloch and Stephen Mitchell. English translation copyright ©1986 by Chana Bloch and Stephen Mitchell. Reprinted by permission of HarperCollins Publishers, Inc.

"Holy Days," by Valerie Worth. In *Poems for Jewish Holidays.* New York: Holiday House. Used by permission of George Worth Bahlke.

"Havdalah," by Carol Adler. In *Poems for Jewish Holidays.* New York: Holiday House. Used by permission of Carol Adler.